EDUCATIONAL PERFORMANCE CONTRACTING

Brookings Studies in
SOCIAL EXPERIMENTATION

EDUCATIONAL PERFORMANCE CONTRACTING

Edward M. Gramlich
Patricia P. Koshel

The Brookings Institution
Washington, D.C.

Library of Congress Cataloging in Publication Data:
Gramlich, Edward M
  Educational performance contracting.

  (Studies in social experimentation)
  Includes bibliographical references.
  1. Performance contracts in education.   2. Educational research.   I. Koshel,
Patricia P., joint author.   II. Title.   III. Series.
LB2806.2.G72   371.1   75-6592

ISBN 0-8157-3239-2

9 8 7 6 5 4 3 2 1

THE BROOKINGS INSTITUTION is an independent organization devoted to nonpartisan research, education, and publication in economics, government, foreign policy, and the social sciences generally. Its principal purposes are to aid in the development of sound public policies and to promote public understanding of issues of national importance.

The Institution was founded on December 8, 1927, to merge the activities of the Institute for Government Research, founded in 1916, the Institute of Economics, founded in 1922, and the Robert Brookings Graduate School of Economics and Government, founded in 1924.

The Board of Trustees is responsible for the general administration of the Institution, while the immediate direction of the policies, program, and staff is vested in the President, assisted by an advisory committee of the officers and staff. The by-laws of the Institution state, "It is the function of the Trustees to make possible the conduct of scientific research, and publication, under the most favorable conditions, and to safeguard the independence of the research staff in the pursuit of their studies and in the publication of the results of such studies. It is not a part of their function to determine, control, or influence the conduct of particular investigations or the conclusions reached."

The President bears final responsibility for the decision to publish a manuscript as a Brookings book or staff paper. In reaching his judgment on the competence, accuracy, and objectivity of each study, the President is advised by the director of the appropriate research program and weighs the views of a panel of expert outside readers who report to him in confidence on the quality of the work. Publication of a work signifies that it is deemed to be a competent treatment worthy of public consideration; such publication does not imply endorsement of conclusions or recommendations contained in the study.

The Institution maintains its position of neutrality on issues of public policy in order to safeguard the intellectual freedom of the staff. Hence interpretations or conclusions in Brookings publications should be understood to be solely those of the author or authors and should not be attributed to the Institution, to its trustees, officers, or other staff members, or to the organizations that support its research.

Foreword

For the past five years the federal government has conducted experiments with alternative social policies to gauge the success or failure of different approaches more effectively than was possible with the somewhat haphazard trial-and-error methods of past decades. The information thus gathered can help to improve programs before they are established and operated on a wide scale, or can lead to a decision to abandon those that do not appear promising. Though potentially of great value, social experiments are still new and imperfect. They generate controversy over design, measurement, and interpretation of results. Hence it is opportune to examine the projects carried out so far to see what lessons can be learned. This study deals with the experiment in educational performance contracting conducted by the Office of Economic Opportunity in the 1970–71 school year.

One objective of the OEO project was to find out whether a private educational firm could teach academically underprivileged children to read and write better than the local public school could. Another was to find out how successfully the pecuniary incentive system operates in education. If firms—or teachers—were paid more as their students learned more, would they do a better job of teaching? The official finding—that the private companies did not seem to teach better than the public schools—was published in 1972, and much methodological and legal controversy has simmered over it ever since. In large measure, the arguments have involved apparent defects in design—whether the experiment was begun too precipitately, covered too short a time span, employed too narrow a range of measurement instruments, or did not allow for a statistically valid comparison of test score gains. Edward M. Gramlich and Patricia P. Koshel examine each of these questions as they describe the design and operation of the experiment. They evaluate the significance of the criticisms and suggest how future experiments might avoid similar difficulties. In general, the authors agree with the official verdict and the broadly negative OEO assessment of performance contracting; but they also point to serious, and in some cases inexcusable, defects in experimental technique.

Edward Gramlich is a senior fellow in the Brookings Economic Studies program; Patricia Koshel is assistant to the director of the National Institute of Education and a former member of the Brookings associated staff. Both were employed by OEO at the time of the experiment. Though neither was officially involved in its operation, they benefited greatly from discussions with those who were, especially John O. Wilson, director of the Division of Planning, Research, and Evaluation; Thomas K. Glennan, Jr., assistant director; Jeffry S. Schiller, director of the Experimental Research Division; Charles B. Stalford, project manager; and Judith A. Glotzer, assistant project manager. They also gained much from interviews with Charles L. Blaschke, Peter G. Briggs, John W. Evans, Edward B. Glassman, Rosemarie C. Lesieur, and Mary M. Lile, all of whom were indirectly involved in the experiment or in performance contracting. They are grateful to the project directors and staff at the twenty sites at which the experiment was conducted for their willingness to be interviewed by telephone, and particularly to Joan M. Webster of Grand Rapids, Michigan, who allowed them to observe a performance contracting classroom in operation. Janet S. Taylor, Hiram Brett, and Phillip J. Spevak assisted in research at various stages of the project; John E. Brandl, Peter G. Briggs, John W. Evans, Irwin Garfinkel, Henry M. Levin, Alice M. Rivlin, Iris C. Rotberg, Marshall S. Smith, Charles B. Stalford, P. Michael Timpane, and John O. Wilson made helpful comments on early drafts; Kathryn Breen and Janet Fain typed the manuscript; Barbara P. Haskins edited it; and Evelyn P. Fisher and Marjorie Kessler verified its factual content.

This is the first book in the Brookings series of Studies in Social Experimentation. The series, which is under the guidance of the Brookings Panel on Social Experimentation (a list of whose members appears on p. xiii) and is supported by a grant from the Edna McConnell Clark Foundation, assesses the usefulness of experiments as a way of increasing knowledge about the effects of domestic social policies and programs of the federal government.

The views expressed here are those of the authors and should not be attributed to any of the persons whose assistance is acknowledged above; to the trustees, officers or other staff members of the Brookings Institution; to the National Institute of Education; or to the Edna McConnell Clark Foundation.

KERMIT GORDON
President

January 1975
Washington, D.C.

Contents

xi

Tables

Figure

xiii

1. Introduction

A widespread response to the real or imagined failure of many social action programs has been to call for more experimentation. Government decisionmakers are being urged to test new policies before they are introduced and existing policies to see how well they work. Such experiments should make it easier to determine if programs should be restructured to improve performance, or whether new approaches should be adopted.

Of course the idea of experimenting with alternative policies is not new. Firms, community groups, governments, and other policymaking bodies have long tried programs on a small scale before making broader policy changes. The national government has also encouraged the development of small and innovative projects both in the antipoverty and foreign aid programs. But the idea of conducting systematic experiments is in many ways quite different from the traditional approach of simply trying things out on a small scale. The policies under investigation are generally national policies that may work in different ways in different places and for different groups. Thus the national social policy experiments have to be much larger and more comprehensive than local trials: at a minimum they must include various demographic groups in various regions. Since such experiments are bigger, they receive more attention and take longer than local ventures. There has also been a more serious attempt in most national social experiments to satisfy the scientific requirements of experimentation—to include control groups explicitly in the design of the experiment, to assign different policy packages to persons or groups randomly, and to try to measure success and failure more precisely.[1]

1. Alice M. Rivlin in *Systematic Thinking for Social Action* (Brookings Institution, 1971, p. 87) discusses the differences between what she calls "random innovation" and "systematic experimentation."

1

One of the areas in which the federal government is beginning to conduct such experiments is in the education of underprivileged children. While there will never be agreement on exactly when a field study qualifies as an experiment, the first project that satisfied most of the requirements began in 1968, when the Department of Health, Education, and Welfare (HEW) instituted planned variations in both its Head Start and Follow Through programs. These variations were designed to make it possible to compare several alternative approaches of providing educational and social services for these children.[2] A second attempt, in some ways more rigorous in its experimental design, came a short time later with an Office of Economic Opportunity (OEO) project in educational performance contracting. In this project the educational performance of private firms operating under incentive contracts—which rewarded them more the more children learned—was compared to that of normal public schools. Additional experiments providing incentives for teachers and parents were undertaken by the Office of Education (OE), and still others are in the planning stage at the newly formed National Institute of Education.

These projects have raised a series of questions about how field experiments might be used to improve education. Since educational policy in the United States is made not only by the federal government but also by fifty state governments and thousands of local school boards, the first question is how the federal government should determine the most relevant areas for experimentation. A second question concerns educational objectives. It is becoming increasingly apparent that educational policymakers at different levels of government still have not agreed on basic goals: whether the educational system should impart knowledge, assist in social and emotional development, teach children how to behave, how to live happily, and how to earn high incomes in later life—or whether it should provide some combination of all of these objectives. Without agreement on goals, it is difficult to measure success and failure of educational experiments, or to tell whether an existing

2. Head Start, launched in 1965, was a program to help preschool children from deprived homes attain the same level of vocabulary and cognitive skills as their middle-class counterparts. Follow Through was an effort in 1967–68 to find ways to continue special education for these children in kindergarten and the first three grades of elementary school. The planned variations experiment is being evaluated in a Brookings research study by Alice M. Rivlin and P. Michael Timpane.

educational system or instructional program is being implemented as efficiently and effectively as it should be.

Finally, there are a number of other considerations involved in large-scale field experiments. Does the necessity of operating in the real world force unavoidable compromises in the experimental design? Does the experiment get unwarranted positive or negative publicity? Are there political or time pressures that unduly compromise the experiment? What are the ethics of using human subjects to test policies that by definition have unknown effects? Until the federal government can answer these questions satisfactorily, it may be wasting its money on large-scale experiments.

This study explores these issues in relation to one completed social experiment in education: the OEO project in educational performance contracting. The monograph examines the experiment from the initial phase—its design, operation, and analysis. It then asks what was learned; whether the experiment satisfactorily answered the questions it raised, whether it should have tried to answer additional questions or different questions, how it could have been better, and how similar experiments in the future should be conducted. Although the study is not the first to review this particular project, it is the first that looks at the experience from the perspective of evaluating not only performance contracting but also its lessons regarding the technique of social experimentation.[3]

Chapter 2 discusses the initial rationale for the project and how it affected the experimental design and the selection of contractors, school districts, and students. Chapter 3 investigates certain problems encountered in the operation of the experiment, such as the companies' programs and their readiness for a real-world test, difficulties in launching the experiment in a short period of time, and OEO's attempt to obtain parents' consent. Chapter 4 takes a close look at the results both from

3. Other descriptions of the experiment are: U.S. Office of Economic Opportunity, Office of Planning, Research, and Evaluation, *An Experiment in Performance Contracting: Summary of Preliminary Results,* OEO Pamphlet 3400-5 (1972); OEO, OPRE, *An Experiment in Performance Contracting,* OEO Pamphlet 3400-6 (1972); Battelle Columbus Laboratories, *Final Report on the Office of Economic Opportunity Experiment in Educational Performance Contracting* (Columbus, Ohio: Battelle Memorial Institute, 1972); and Education Turnkey Systems, *Final Report to OEO: Performance Incentive Remedial Education Experiment,* BOO-5114 (Washington, D.C.: Education Turnkey Systems, Inc., 1971).

an overall and a site-by-site basis to see if, on balance, the contractors were more successful as a group than the normal public school programs, which firms were most successful, and if any fared better on certain sub-components of the achievement tests than on others. The nature of any possible ambiguities in the results caused by testing problems or deviations from random selection in certain sites is considered, and the chapter also includes a parallel examination of student attendance to see if there were any differences between the experimental and control groups. Chapter 5 explores the contractual aspects of the experiment: whether the incentive contracting mechanism was a success, whether specific incentives built into the contracts encouraged certain types of teaching or differential focus on certain students, whether any other unanticipated legal or contractual issues arose, and the like. Chapter 6 then discusses the implications of the entire experience, the major problems encountered, their severity, and how they might have been better handled. It concludes by speculating on the value of such large-scale social experiments as a technique for improving understanding of educational problems.

2. Rationale and Structure

The idea of using economic incentives in education is actually very old; it was first tried in the English educational system in the nineteenth century. Beginning in 1863 and lasting for over thirty years, grants to schools were determined by a performance contracting scheme based partly on pupil attainment and partly on attendance. The English experiment with performance contracting was ultimately discontinued because it resulted in low pay and great financial insecurity for teachers, and also because it effectively limited teaching to the subject areas tested. But when interest in a similar concept arose in this country in 1970, there was little recollection of this early English experience.[1]

Initial Rationale

The contemporary setting for the performance contracting experiment was the generally depressing results of evaluations of educational enrichment programs for disadvantaged students. Most investigations of educational innovations, such as those involving class size, training of teachers, time spent on study, or conventional instruction methods, were showing that the changes had relatively little effect on academic achievement. This tradition was supported by the massive and highly publicized Coleman report in 1966, which indicated that neither teacher-pupil ratios nor expenditure per pupil bore any strong relationship to academic achievement,

1. One exception is Jeanette B. Coltham, "Educational Accountability: An English Experiment and Its Outcome," *The University of Chicago School Review*, vol. 81 (November 1972), pp. 15–34. Coltham reports (p. 26) that a schoolmaster of the 1880s wrote: "I declare positively that when one of my backward boys died of bronchitis a few weeks back I felt a measure of relief; for his death would make one failure less." If this remark is to be taken literally, it is a rather striking indication of the financial insecurity of teachers of that era.

and later by the various evaluations of compensatory education programs for academically underprivileged students. The Office of Economic Opportunity (OEO) itself became involved in 1969 with a generally negative evaluation of the long-run educational effects of the popular Head Start program for preschool children.[2]

There was therefore much interest in an early report that the Dorsett Educational Systems, a private firm operating under an incentive contract, had succeeded in doubling and even tripling the normal achievement gains of educationally disadvantaged students in Texarkana, Arkansas.[3] Although the Dorsett program relied heavily on individualized instruction and various audiovisual aids, it was not this aspect of the project that attracted the main interest. The important feature of the Texarkana project was that Dorsett had signed a contract with the school board stipulating that reimbursement should be directly related to students' achievement scores. If the students did not reach a certain

2. The Coleman report refers to the study, James S. Coleman and others, *Equality of Educational Opportunity* (U.S. Government Printing Office, 1966). It was the first attempt on a national scale to measure the performance of schoolchildren by race and socioeconomic group and to compare the conditions under which they were being educated.

The tradition of negative research findings is summarized in J. M. Stephens, *The Process of Schooling: A Psychological Examination* (Holt, Rinehart, and Winston, 1967), chap. 7. Frederick Mosteller and Daniel P. Moynihan (eds.), *On Equality of Educational Opportunity* (Random House, 1972), and Christopher Jencks and others, *Inequality: A Reassessment of the Effect of Family and Schooling in America* (Basic Books, 1972), report on further analyses of the same data. The evaluations of compensatory education can be found in various reports on the program, the most recent of which is Michael J. Wargo and others, *ESEA Title I: A Reanalysis and Synthesis of Evaluation Data from Fiscal Year 1965 through 1970* (Palo Alto, Calif.: American Institutes for Research in the Behavioral Sciences, March 1972). The OEO evaluation of Head Start is Victor Cicarelli and others, *The Impact of Head Start: An Evaluation of the Effects of Head Start on Children's Cognitive and Affective Development* (Westinghouse Learning Corporation and Ohio University, 1969; distributed by Clearinghouse for Federal Scientific and Technical Information, Springfield, Va.). A more recent look at the same data can be found in Burt S. Barnow, *Evaluating Project Head Start,* Discussion Paper 189–73 (University of Wisconsin, Institute for Research on Poverty, 1973).

3. See Martin J. Filogamo, "New Angle on Accountability," *Today's Education,* vol. 59 (May 1970), p. 53, and Stanley Elam, "The Age of Accountability Dawns in Texarkana," *Phi Delta Kappan,* vol. 51 (June 1970), pp. 509, 511–14. These articles report average gains of 2.2 grades in reading and 1.4 grades in mathematics after just sixty hours of Dorsett instruction. Visitors to the site were told of similar results although they were never shown any test data. It is not clear just where these reports originated.

level in a certain period of time, the company would not be reimbursed even for its costs. Because this arrangement rewarded the firm only for successful teaching, it came to be known as a performance contract.

In the Texarkana project students considered by the school to be sufficiently below the average grade levels for their age were put into a special program, operated in vacant classrooms and house trailers near the school, where they were given special instruction by Dorsett. The students "graduated" from the special program as soon as they had improved in their reading and mathematical achievement tests by one grade level. If a student reached this level in eighty instructional hours, Dorsett was to be paid approximately $80, roughly the cost of educating that student. If a student achieved this level sooner, Dorsett would be paid more and make a profit; if later, Dorsett would be paid less and lose; and if a student still had not graduated in 168 hours, Dorsett would get nothing at all. Within certain guidelines, the contracts gave Dorsett wide latitude in terms of numbers of teachers, instructional programs, techniques, equipment, and student incentives. Dorsett's only task was to improve student performance, and it was free to do that in any way it could.[4]

The Texarkana project was visited by educational personnel from every state in the Union and sources there indicate that more than two hundred school districts were thinking seriously of adopting a similar program.[5] More than one hundred did in the 1970–71 school year.[6]

There was also a receptive audience at the federal level. The Texarkana story came out just as President Nixon released an important congressional message on education, which featured the statement that local systems should be held "accountable" for their performance.[7] Similar speeches were being made by many other officials in both the

4. A more complete description of the Texarkana contracts can be found in Robert D. Hamrin, "Performance Contracting in Education: An Economic Analysis of the 1970–71 Office of Economic Opportunity Experiment" (Ph.D. thesis, University of Wisconsin, 1972).

5. Mary M. Lile, the executive administrative assistant for the Texarkana program, provided this information.

6. A list of the districts adopting performance contracting can be found in G. R. Hall and others, *A Guide to Educational Performance Contracting,* R-955/1-HEW (Santa Monica, Calif.: Rand Corporation, 1972), p. 9.

7. *Education for the 1970's: Renewal and Reform,* Message to the Congress by Richard Nixon, President of the United States (March 1970).

Office of Education and OEO.[8] The fact that companies teaching under performance contracts would not be paid unless merited by the results meant that the concept of incentive contracting was ideally suited to the accountability theme. The fact that the companies were private—demonstrating the fruits of free enterprise—made the idea even more attractive to Republican policymakers.

Performance contracting was also appealing to those who felt that teachers should be given sufficient monetary incentive to improve their techniques, focus on disadvantaged students, try new methods, and the like. Teacher salaries were alleged to be based on seniority scales that encouraged teachers to conform and not cause trouble rather than try out new ways of doing things. An institutional change that meant that firms and ultimately their teachers would be paid only according to how well they taught might disrupt this tradition and make it to the firms' advantage to improve their methods. In fact, in the longer run a system of monetary incentives could lead to even more fundamental changes in existing educational systems. Those firms (or teachers) that were successful in teaching underprivileged children (and for that matter all other children) would thrive and expand; those that failed would give up teaching. Local school boards would be given a chance to purchase educational materials on the basis of outputs—the pupils who succeeded—instead of inputs—the number of students, room space, and the like. Boards could choose from competing sources of supply, buy materials from firms with real experience in teaching and a tradition of success, and write incentive contracts that would favor disadvantaged students.

But there was also opposition to the concept. The most vociferous came from the major national teacher organizations. While there was no indication that they were aware of the English experience, they did issue several statements warning of possible financial insecurity for teachers. After all, incentive contracts do not guarantee anybody's pay, they only make it possible to earn more if students do well, which the teachers realized was probably very unlikely. Teachers also undoubtedly felt threatened by the specter of private firms competing for their jobs and

8. "Experiments in Education" (address by Donald Rumsfeld, San Francisco Chamber of Commerce, September 23, 1970; processed); and Leon Lessinger, "Engineering Accountability for Results in Public Education," in J. A. Mecklenburger, J. A. Wilson, and R. W. Hostrop (eds.), *Learning C.O.D.: Can the Schools Buy Success?* (Hamden, Conn.: Shoe String Press, 1972).

by some officials' early speeches that may have been more challenging and contentious than necessary.[9]

This qualified interest in performance contracting, the President's plea for accountability, and another theme in the same presidential message on education that the government should not adopt policies until there was assurance they would work finally led to the decision to conduct a social experiment in educational performance contracting.[10] OEO, at that time being transformed from an organization that actually operated national programs to one mainly interested in research, evaluation, and program development, seemed the appropriate agency in which to house such an experiment. OEO was interested and experienced in the area of social experimentation—having recently begun a widely publicized income maintenance experiment.[11] It was interested in performance contracting,[12] and it was less beholden to the teacher organizations and the educational establishment generally than the Office of Education might have been. It also had enough money to begin the project right away. Rigorous evaluation of social programs had become the vogue at OEO, and a controlled experiment with performance contracting looked like an ideal project.

The Goals

An experiment to test the idea of performance contracting could be designed in two quite different ways. At one extreme, the long-run organizational advantages of introducing market incentives into education could have been examined through an experiment where private firms or teachers negotiated incentive contracts with school boards that allowed them time to alter their methods in response to successes or failures and also even to expand or contract their business and enter or leave the industry. This type of experiment would feature incentive con-

9. American Federation of Teachers, "The Performance Contract: Innovation or Hucksterism?" (AFT, undated pamphlet; processed) is one sample of the teacher opposition to performance contracting.

10. *Education for the 1970's.*

11. See, for example, Daniel P. Moynihan, *The Politics of a Guaranteed Income: The Nixon Administration and the Family Assistance Plan* (Random House, 1973), p. 191.

12. See Rumsfeld, "Experiments in Education."

tracts, no OEO control of teaching method, and it would presumably last for several years.[13] At the other extreme, the more immediate advantages of teaching students by new and innovative methods introduced by private firms—and possibly also by some teachers—could have been examined in an experiment that did not incorporate incentive contracting and that lasted for a much shorter time. The methods of instruction used in both experimental and control classrooms would have to be determined beforehand, maintained throughout the experiment, and carefully documented.

As it turned out, the OEO experiment was a generally unsatisfactory mixture of both ingredients. It featured incentive contracts whereby both private firms—and in a few cases local teachers—were paid according to their students' progress. Though there was an attempt to enroll firms using somewhat different approaches, these firms were free to alter their procedures during the course of the experiment if they felt such changes would make their program more successful. OEO neither restricted nor monitored the instructional methods of the schools in the control groups, which were free to teach in ways every bit as new and innovative as those used in the experimental classrooms.

The experiment also fell far short of a test of an educational incentive system. Because it would have been costly to conduct a multiyear experiment (the annual cost would have been about $6 million), because it would have been politically embarrassing to allow private firms several years to accomplish what they said they could do in one year, and because many school boards wanted results quickly, OEO made a provisional decision to limit the experiment to one academic year.[14] This one-year limit meant that while the firms did have time within the experiment to correct obvious instructional problems, there clearly was no time to test many of the supposed longer-term advantages of performance contracting.

Thus the experiment was really a test of the learning technology and management abilities of the outside private firms as of 1970, and of the value of profit incentives in the short run. This ambivalent approach was not very satisfactory from the perspective of either those interested

13. An experiment of this type has been recommended by Dennis R. Young, "Evaluation of Organizational Change: The Case of Performance Contracting in Education," Working Paper 1205-05 (Urban Institute, August 1972; processed).

14. There was some feeling within OEO that the experiment should have been planned for a longer time, but by the middle of the first year of operation sufficient problems had already been encountered that there was no enthusiasm for extending it.

in organizational change or those interested in teaching method; but the project did provide at least some information on both aspects. It was also of value to the thousands of local school boards who in 1970 were faced with the decision of whether or not they should sign up with an outside contractor: if they could await the outcome of the experiment in a year, they would have much better information on which to base such a choice.

The Design

In more specific terms, the experiment was to be both general and rigorous in its design. To make the experiment broadly applicable, OEO decided to enroll a number of private firms (six) in a number of sites (three per contractor), and to have the contractors teach in a number of grades in both elementary and junior high school (first, second, third, seventh, eighth, and ninth grades.) Late in the planning period, OEO included two more sites where incentive contracts were signed with local teacher organizations contracted to conduct programs offering incentives only, thus giving an opportunity to determine the separate contributions of private firms and incentive contracts to any educational successes.

The rigorous aspect of the experiment was seen in the attempt to make careful comparisons between experimental and control groups. Large numbers of control students were included in the experiment, in the same grade and at the same site (but not the same school) as the experimental students. They were selected from similar populations of underprivileged students and tested with the same tests on the same dates as the participating students.

Procedures

The experiment was conducted entirely within the regular public school system. In those schools designated as control schools, everything was to run normally except that 100 of the most academically deficient students in the first, second, and third grades of elementary school and in the seventh, eighth, and ninth grades of junior high were to be tested in reading and mathematics skills before their schooling began in the fall and again when their school year ended in the spring.

They were to be given a questionnaire for their parents on attitude and family characteristics. There was to be no OEO control over the length of time students spent in reading and mathematics instruction in these schools, though the reasonable expectation was that students would spend about one hour a day on each subject.[15]

In the experimental schools 150 of the least successful students in the same grades were designated for the experiment, with the 100 who were most deficient initially assigned to the experimental group and the other 50 to a replacement group. The 100 participating students in each grade were taken out of their regular classrooms and instructed by the companies in specially remodeled classrooms in the same school, for one hour a day in both reading and mathematics. If any of these students were to drop out during the school year, their positions in the experimental program were to be filled by students from the replacement group so that the firm's total payment could be computed on the basis of 100 students. Students in the experimental and replacement groups were all to be pretested in the fall and post-tested in the spring, at the same time as the students in the control groups; the students who were to replace those who left were also to be tested whenever they joined the experimental program. All students in the experimental and replacement groups were to be given the same questionnaire for their parents as students in the control groups.

The Tests

In order to avoid the possibility of contractors "teaching to the tests," which was later alleged to have happened in Texarkana,[16] OEO adopted

15. The General Accounting Office (GAO) criticized the OEO experiment in May 1973 for failing to control the instructional time spent on reading and mathematics in the control schools (see *Evaluation of the Office of Economic Opportunity's Performance Contracting Experiment,* Report to the Congress by the Comptroller General of the United States, B-130515 [1973], p. 19). The idea of this experiment was not to compare efficiency per minute in the classrooms run by contractors and control schools, but to see whether contractors operating under these conditions could outperform the normal public schools. Although one could argue that there should have been some restriction of the curriculum of the control schools, information compiled by the Education Turnkey Systems, the management support contractor, indicates that there was little difference in instructional time between the experimental and control schools (see Charles B. Stalford, "Analysis of Program Costs," in U.S. Office of Economic Opportunity, Office of Planning, Research, and Evaluation, *An Experiment in Performance Contracting,* OEO Pamphlet 3400-6 [1972], pp. 172–73).

16. Dorsett was reported to have included certain test items in its instructional

a rather elaborate testing procedure for the experimental group. In the beginning and at the end of the school year these students were to be tested twice: once to determine the size of the company performance payments and once to evaluate progress in relation to the control schools. The identity of both sets of tests was to be concealed from the contractors (as it was from personnel in the control schools), although the contractors were asked to suggest reading and mathematical achievement tests that might be used in the experiment.[17] The evaluation achievement tests (the same as those given to the control students) were given to students in the experiment first so as to prevent "practice effects." The payments tests, for which there would be the greatest incentive to teach to the tests, were given on the following day, with the additional safeguard that each grade was given three different forms of this particular test, assigned randomly to different students.[18]

Because the participating students had been deliberately chosen from among those below the national norms of achievement in relation to age and grade, in every case OEO used pre- and post-tests for a population of students approximately one grade below the actual grade being tested.

The Contracts

The incentive contracts were similar to those used in Texarkana, though with one important difference. Instead of basing payment on

---

materials. Thereupon, the Texarkana school board tried to withhold Dorsett's payments. It was ultimately enjoined from doing so by the U.S. District Court in Texarkana, Arkansas, although the court proceedings did establish that 6 to 7 percent of the test items were "compromised." See National School Public Relations Association, *Education U.S.A.* (Washington, D.C., February 26, 1973), p. 140.

17. The contractors suggested several tests in reply to initial OEO queries, most of which were ultimately used in the experiment. This made the contractors' charge that OEO had selected tests unfairly somewhat perplexing (see *An Experiment in Performance Contracting*, OEO Pamphlet 3400-6, p. 231). Additional information on the tests that were used can be found in Jeffry S. Schiller and Ellen P. Murdoch, "Implications of Using Standardized Tests in Performance Contracting," in *An Experiment in Performance Contracting,* pp. 51–108.

18. If firms cared only about how well they did on this particular trial with performance contracting, they would presumably only try to cheat on the payments test. But if they also cared about how the performance contracting firms as a group and their own firm in particular stood up on the overall evaluation, they would also presumably try to cheat on the evaluation tests. However, there were no reports of such behavior in the experiment.

how fast students attained a certain prespecified gain in achievement scores, the OEO contracts rewarded firms on the basis of how much students gained in one academic year. Any other ground rules would have made it impossible, or at least very difficult, to compare students in the experimental and control groups. If participating students dropped out during the year and their places were filled by replacement students, the gains for contractual purposes were to be spliced together.[19]

Although each of the six firms in the experiment negotiated and signed separate incentive contracts with OEO, these contracts were similar both in basic outline and the underlying details.[20] In general, the contracts were quite unfavorable to the firms, though that appeared to be due more to the firms' confidence and desire to publicize their performance contracting operations rather than to OEO's hard bargaining. The typical contract, summarized in Figure 2-1, stipulated that a firm would get no payment at all for any student who failed to gain one grade equivalent unit.[21] There was to be a lump sum payment for every student who reached this level; the average payment was $75—or approximately 43 percent of the contractors' actual costs per student for instruction and administration. In addition, contractors were paid an average of $8 for each student's gain of 0.1 grade equivalent unit above 1.0. The ceiling on the government's liability was to average $200 times the number of students in the class-room, or 15 percent more than the typical firm's total cost.[22] In addition,

19. In fact, this often turned out to be difficult to do and other methods of adjustment often were used (see chapter 5).

20. These contracts were technically signed with the local school boards in each of the experimental sites, though OEO negotiated all contracts and, through a separate agreement, reimbursed these districts for any costs incurred.

21. How many questions a student answers correctly on a test (his raw score) does not indicate his achievement in relation to other students. The common method of comparison is to use students' grade equivalent scores. These are calculated by administering one test to several successive grades at a particular time in the school year and determining what the median scores are for the various grades in the norm sample. A student's grade equivalent score is the grade level of students for which the median score equaled his raw score. A student may be in third grade, for example, but his reading performance—his grade equivalent score—may be that of a second-grade child in the second month of the school year: 2.2.

22. This ceiling was negotiated under the assumption that it would limit the firms' profit to 20 percent of their costs. The eventual limit was lower because actual instructional costs were higher than the firms had anticipated. Even 15 percent is higher than is normally allowed in government contracts, but other contracts do not generally entail such high risks.

25 percent of a contractor's maximum pay was to be based on the results of five interim performance objective (IPO) tests, to be given during the course of the school year to measure students' mastery of curricular skills specific to the contractor's program. Even if a student earned the full payment for these IPO tests, he would still have to gain 1.6 grade equivalent units during the year (about two and one-half times what past performance indicated as typical for these students) for the contractor to break even.

Figure 2-1. Typical Educational Performance Incentive Contract, 1970–71 Experiment

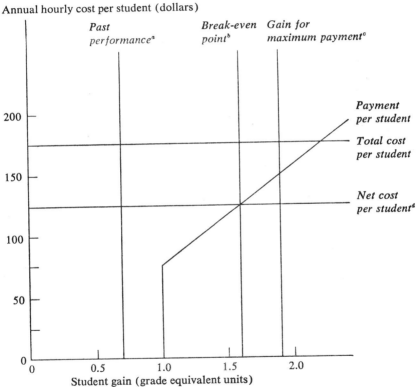

Source: Charles B. Stalford, "Contractual Procedures." in U.S. Office of Economic Opportunity, Office of Planning, Research, and Evaluation, *An Experiment in Performance Contracting*, OEO Pamphlet 3400-6 (1972), p. 136.

a. Average past performance for a like sample of students.
b. The gain required by a student for the incentive payment to cover costs.
c. The gain required by all students in a class for the contractor to earn the maximum payment.
d. The total cost per student net of maximum payment for the interim performance objective tests.

In fact, all students in the entire class would have to gain an average of 1.9 grade equivalent units for the firm to earn its maximum payment, which would exceed its total cost by only 15 percent.[23] Thus there was much for the contractors to lose, and little for them to gain, in these contracts—a fact which later caused both the contractors and OEO serious problems in negotiating the final settlements of these contracts.

Selection of Firms, School Districts, and Students

The Office of Economic Opportunity used the standard government procurement procedure in selecting firms for the experiment. In April 1970, it announced the experiment in the *Commerce Business Daily,* asking respondents for statements of general capability, teaching experience, and their proposed approach.[24] Thirty-one firms responded to this initial request. After a screening that eliminated firms that showed little prospect of success and those whose response did not address the issues raised in the OEO solicitations, the remaining twelve respondents were grouped into categories according to the intensity of their use of machines and student incentives. Within each category, the one or two firms that seemed to promise the highest benefit-cost ratio were selected. In most cases OEO was able to choose the firm that seemed most competent within a category, though a few firms were eliminated because their costs of instruction were very high.[25] Table 2-1 lists firms finally selected, along with their educational approach, teacher-student ratios, and use of paraprofessionals.

23. The calculation is as follows: the average level of firms' instructional cost is computed (from data in *An Experiment in Performance Contracting,* OEO Pamphlet 3400-6, Table II, p. 174, and Table VII, pp. 183–84) as the sum of instructional cost plus administrative costs. It averaged $175 an hour per student for both subjects in both elementary and junior high schools. If the firm received the average maximum IPO payment of $50 per student (Table III, p. 136), it would need to make $125 per student to break even. This entails a lump sum payment of $75 and extra payments of $50, or $8 per 0.1 grade equivalent unit gain in excess of 1.0 (or 1.6 grade unit gain). For the firm to make the average maximum payment of $200 for all students (ibid.), all students would have to gain $200 − $50 (for IPO tests) − $75 (lump sum payment) = $75 in extra payments, or 0.9 gain in excess of unity. All of these figures are averages; the situation would be slightly different for each contractor and in each grade.
24. See *Commerce Business Daily,* Issue PSA-5053 (April 27, 1970), p. 4.
25. This information was obtained from project manager Charles B. Stalford.

Table 2-1. Performance Contracting Firms, by Educational Approach,
Teacher-Student Ratios, and Use of Paraprofessionals, 1970–71 School Year

Firm	Use of machines	Use of incentives to students	Teacher-student ratio	Use of parapro-fessionals (percent of staff)
Learning Foundations	High	High	1:5	100
Westinghouse Learning Corporation	Moderate	Moderate	1:12	80
Quality Educational Development Corporation	Moderate	Moderate	1:13	50
Alpha Learning Systems	Low	High	1:15	40
Singer/Graflex	Low	Moderate	1:20	40
Plan Education Centers	Low	None	1:5	50

Source: U.S. Office of Economic Opportunity, summary tabulation of results of OEO questionnaires sent to project directors at each educational performance contracting site.

School districts were chosen in a similar manner. The management support firm already under contract to OEO, Education Turnkey Systems, Inc., sent an invitation to participate to over 200 school districts that were apparently interested in performance contracting. The 163 districts that responded were sent a project application form; 77 of these districts applied for participation in the project. The latter were then screened according to the following five criteria:

1. The district qualified for assistance under Title I of the Elementary and Secondary Education Act; that is, at least 80 percent of its population had poverty-level incomes.

2. According to the national norms, the students were deficient in reading and mathematics.

3. The district was large enough to provide the requisite numbers of students in both elementary and secondary grades.[26]

4. The district had recent, valid, and reliable achievement test data available so that schools and students could be readily assigned to experimental and control groups.

5. There were no political, social, or economic problems in the area that might interfere with the project.

Twenty-two districts met these criteria and represented a reasonable geographic, demographic, and urban-rural distribution. Four dropped out

26. This criterion was waived in some instances to allow small rural districts to participate in the experiment. Three sites had only 75 students per grade in the control group instead of 100, and in two of these sites the control groups were located in nearby school districts.

Table 2-2. Individual Site Characteristics in the Educational Performance Contracting Experiment, by Contractor, 1970–71 School Year

Firm	Site of school district	Region	Size of area,[a] 1970	Predominant race or nationality of students	Per capita income of students' families, 1970
Learning Foundations	Bronx, New York	Northeast	Large urban	Black; Puerto Rican	$1,300
	Jacksonville, Florida	Southeast	Large urban	Black	800
	Hammond, Indiana	North Central	Medium urban	White; black	1,700
Westinghouse Learning Corporation	Philadelphia, Pennsylvania	Northeast	Large urban	Black	700
	Fresno, California	Southwest	Medium urban	White; Chicano	1,200
	Las Vegas, Nevada	Southwest	Medium urban	White; black	1,700
Quality Educational Development Corporation	Dallas, Texas	South Central	Large urban	Black	600
	Anchorage, Alaska	Northwest	Small urban	White; Eskimo; black	2,600[b]
	Rockland, Maine	Northeast	Rural	White	1,500
Alpha Learning Systems	Grand Rapids, Michigan	North Central	Medium urban	White; black	1,400
	Hartford, Connecticut	Northeast	Medium urban	Black	800
	Taft, Texas	Southwest	Rural	Chicano	600
Singer/Graflex	Seattle, Washington	Northwest	Large urban	White; black	1,700
	Portland, Maine	Northeast	Small urban	White	1,400
	McComb, Mississippi	South Central	Rural	White; black	800
Plan Education Centers	Wichita, Kansas	Mid-Central	Medium urban	White; black	1,400
	Athens, Georgia	Southeast	Rural	White; black	1,100
	Selmer, Tennessee	South Central	Rural	White	1,200
Local teacher organization[c]	Stockton, California	Southwest	Medium urban	White; black; Chicano	900
	Mesa, Arizona	Southwest	Small urban	White; Indian; Chicano	800

Sources: Battelle Columbus Laboratories, *Final Report on the Office of Economic Opportunity Experiment in Educational Performance Contracting* (Columbus, Ohio: Battelle Memorial Institute, 1972), p. 28; U.S. Office of Economic Opportunity, Office of Planning, Research, and Evaluation, *A Demonstration of Incentives in Education*, OEO Pamphlet 3400-7 (1972); Education Turnkey Systems, *Performance Incentive Remedial Education Experiment*, Final Report to the Office of Economic Opportunity, BOO-5114 (Washington, D.C.: Education Turnkey Systems, Inc., 1971), p. 14; and data provided by OEO.

a. Large urban indicates school district in a city with a population in excess of 500,000; medium urban, a population between 100,000 and 500,000; small urban, a population between 40,000 and 100,000; and rural, a rural district with a population less than 40,000.

b. The high figure for Anchorage is misleading because living costs are higher there.

c. The experiment involved incentive payments for local teachers.

during negotiations. The remaining eighteen districts were matched with the six contractors by OEO, again to ensure that each firm was teaching in a reasonably diverse range of districts.[27] Later, two other sites were selected by a separate process when it was decided to include teachers in the experiment involving incentives only. The final pairings, along with other demographic information on the districts, are given in Table 2-2.

Individual schools within the districts were eligible for the experiment if they were among the most academically deficient schools in the district that met the criteria for federal assistance under Title I of the Elementary and Secondary Education Act, if they had a large enough pool of students to satisfy the requirements of the experiment, and if they had no other special programs or performance contracts in operation. Since the contractors were arguing that their programs were primarily remedial in nature, and since OEO was interested in how well the contractors' programs would educate academically underprivileged students, the most academically deficient schools in a district were typically assigned by OEO to the experimental groups and the next most deficient to the control groups. In certain cases this order was reversed if the most deficient school was not large enough to provide the additional fifty replacement students per grade, or if there were any other reasons (according to the criteria established) for not using certain schools.[28]

Finally, within each experimental and control school the students judged to be most deficient academically were selected for the experiment. Generally, this assessment was based on scores of achievement tests for reading and mathematics given within the previous two years, but in some cases previous grades, IQ scores, or more informal teacher assessments had to be substituted, especially for first grade students, who did not have previous achievement rankings.

Problems with the Selection Procedures

There has been much critical comment regarding the selection procedures OEO used in the experiment, both for firms and for schools and

27. A more complete description of this selection process can be found in Education Turnkey Systems, *Performance Incentive Remedial Education Experiment,* Final Report to the Office of Economic Opportunity, BOO-5114 (Washington, D.C.: Education Turnkey Systems, Inc., 1971), chap. 1.

28. The report of Education Turnkey Systems, in *Performance Incentive,* p. 23, contains a list of some of these difficulties.

students. For example, OEO picked a sample of six firms that was reasonably representative in certain important aspects of the universe of all firms interested in participating in the experiment. But a sample of firms is by definition not the entire universe, and there was at least one firm, Behavioral Research Laboratories, that was sufficiently disappointed in not being selected that it appealed to the General Accounting Office. The latter's audit of the experiment probably reflected its reaction to this complaint because it maintained (without any evidence that firms not chosen would have done better) that OEO's procedures for selecting firms were inadequate from a contracting standpoint.[29] It is impossible to tell whether other firms would have done any better than those chosen, but it is highly unlikely that the OEO would not have chosen at least some of the best qualified firms. If anything, it seems more reasonable to argue that OEO selected its firms with more expertise and care than would be exercised by the typical school board.

There has been less criticism of procedures for selecting school districts. The experiment dealt with underachieving students in academically deficient school districts. This makes it impossible to compare the experiment's results with results for other populations of students, such as high achievers or even the poor students in school districts of higher academic standing. With such a large experiment, however, there were undoubtedly enough students of average ability that any generalizations about the findings should not be totally wide of the mark. The results apply, of course, only to those districts that want to try performance contracting—not to those that have such contracts forced upon them. Nonetheless, it may still be difficult to relate the experiment's results even to districts that want to try using outside firms because they would negotiate their own contracts whereas in the experiment the OEO matched the companies with the sites and made many of the arrangements.

Within a district, schools were not able to volunteer but were assigned to experimental or control status by OEO. Had that not been done, it would have been impossible to tell whether any differences between students in the experimental and control groups reflected real differences in treatment or simply the fact that experimental schools and participating students may have liked performance contracting better, chosen it voluntarily, and tried harder to make it work than other students and schools. The latter effect, known as self-selection bias, has been a

29. *Evaluation of the Office of Economic Opportunity's Performance Contracting Experiment*, p. 44.

problem in many previous evaluations of education and manpower programs.

Even though schools were assigned to experimental and control status by OEO, because the students and schools in the experiment were not selected at random but were slightly more deficient academically than those in control groups (thus violating a basic canon of experimentation), the selection process did draw critical comment.[30] The criticism, originally raised in Campbell and Erlebacher's attack on OEO's Head Start evaluation, was that actual pretest scores can never provide a perfect correction for the initial disadvantage of students in the experimental group because they do not measure true ability perfectly.[31] It can be shown, however, that if measurement error on achievement tests is random, so that pretest scores do measure true ability well on average, it is possible to develop and apply corrections for any biases due to unequal pretest abilities (see chapter 4). These correction factors, which are very small because the initial differences in pretest abilities between experimental and control schools were themselves rather small, should eliminate most of the bias due to lack of randomization.[32]

Thus the problems with the selection procedures do not appear to be overwhelming. The procedure for firms need not necessarily have enlisted the best, but it is hard to argue that it systematically excluded them, and there is no evidence that this occurred. School districts were not selected for the experiment randomly, but if one takes the reasonable posture that the experiment is only relevant for districts interested enough in performance contracting to want to do it on their own, and for districts with large concentrations of disadvantaged students, the results should be unbiased and appropriate. The assignment of schools to experimental and control status also deviated slightly from a random

30. See Gary Saretsky, "The OEO P.C. Experiment and the John Henry Effect," *Phi Delta Kappan,* vol. 53 (May 1972), pp. 579–81.

31. Donald T. Campbell and Albert Erlebacher, "How Regression Artifacts in Quasi-Experimental Evaluations Can Mistakenly Make Compensatory Education Look Harmful," in Jerome Hellmuth (ed.), *Compensatory Education: A National Debate,* vol. 3 of *Disadvantaged Child* (Brunner/Mazel, 1970).

32. See Irwin Garfinkel and Edward M. Gramlich, "A Statistical Analysis of the OEO Experiment in Educational Performance Contracting," *Journal of Human Resources,* vol. 8 (Summer 1973), pp. 275–305 (also published in OEO Pamphlet 3400-6, cited above, pp. 1–50), for a discussion of this correction. A more general treatment of the problem is given in Arthur S. Goldberger, "Selection Bias in Evaluating Treatment Effects: Some Formal Illustrations," Discussion Paper 123-72 (Institute for Research on Poverty, 1972).

process, but fortunately these schools were not allowed to choose for themselves—the problem that can cause the worst difficulties—and fortunately there are statistical ways of removing the main problem caused by imperfectly matching schools and students in the two groups. A careful interpretation of the results of the experiment can, in other words, overcome most of the statistical difficulties likely to be present.

3. The Experiment in Action

Field experiments such as the performance contracting project are very difficult to organize and manage. Firms and school districts must be enrolled, instructional programs set up, project administrators installed, the cooperation of school personnel enlisted, and tests given. While many of these tasks went smoothly in the performance contracting experiment, many did not and could have been responsible for certain ambiguities in interpreting the final results. In order to better understand what happened, therefore, it is necessary to take a close look at the actual events of the field experiment. This chapter first describes the companies' programs and how well they were implemented, then the details of launching the experiment, the attempt of the Office of Economic Opportunity to obtain parents' consent for students in the experimental group, and finally a few miscellaneous disturbances that made the results at some sites particularly suspect.

The Companies' Programs

The general theme underlying the instructional programs of the six companies was to increase student motivation. All programs attempted to avoid the allegedly stifling traditional classroom atmosphere where the teacher worked with the entire group, students were at attention, and desks were neatly lined up in straight rows. The performance contracting programs instead featured individually prescribed lesson plans, students working on their own projects at their own pace, a much more casual classroom atmosphere, and also much noisier classrooms. Rather than having one fully licensed teacher in every classroom, many of the companies tried to replace and supplement these teachers as much as possible with aides, paraprofessionals, and a range of teaching machines,

23

audiovisual tutors, and cassette recorders. The firms also insisted on re-furbishing the classroom facilities with small tables and chairs or learn-ing carrels, which could be grouped in many ways depending on the day's activities; sometimes there were carpets to cut down noise.

There were important differences among the programs of the six companies. They differed, for instance, in their reliance on certified teachers rather than paraprofessionals and machines (see Table 2-2). They also differed in their philosophy of rewarding students for com-pleting lessons—some firms such as Learning Foundations and Alpha Learning Systems made extensive use of tangible incentives, such as toys, small games, and candy bars, to maintain student interest in the instructional program; others, such as Quality Educational Development Corporation, attempted to provide intangible incentives like free time to play educational games, listen to music, read, or carry on other activi-ties; while still others, such as Plan Education Centers, thought that the sheer satisfaction of learning was sufficient recompense and did not use tangible student rewards at all. The companies also differed in the extent to which they relied on their own or on commercially available instructional programs, and in the degree to which their programs relied on the imagination and expertise of the teachers.

While the firms were initially chosen partly because they planned to do things differently, the basic idea behind the experiment was that they were free to modify their programs, and as the year went on they did. In some cases changes were made deliberately, while in other cases circumstances forced the changes. Many of the firms that relied heavily on their own instructional programs were not able to supply these materials on schedule and had to permit their teachers to use available commercial materials. Many of the firms that relied on teach-ing machines and other hardware could not maintain their equipment and had to resort to less capital-intensive ways of teaching. In Las Vegas, for example, Westinghouse Learning Corporation had to aban-don its reel-to-reel tape recorders when it found that students learned how to erase the tapes and record obscenities. The programs that relied on teacher rewards could not make the incentive payments when it became apparent that they generated too much hostility. The programs that relied heavily on tangible student incentives could not keep this up either when the rewards failed to arrive in time—Learning Foundations kept certain students in Jacksonville waiting for theirs until October of the following year. On the other side, the programs of the Plan Education Centers, which relied to an unusual degree on the inspiration of its local teachers, became more structured as the year progressed. Although broad generalizations are dangerous, most of the programs seemed to gravitate toward a somewhat more individualized approach than those in the traditional classrooms, with some—but not exclusive— use of paraprofessionals and teaching machines, a limited use of tangible student incentives but fairly heavy reliance on the intangible incentive of free time, no incentive payments for teachers, and general dependence on commercially available instructional materials.[1]

One indispensable element both in shaping the character of the firms' programs and in their degree of success was the caliber of the local project director. This person, usually someone who had been an administrator or teacher in the district, was responsible for running the project, keeping records, assisting the firms, and stepping in when things did not seem to be going well. Some of the more successful project directors in fact took on so much responsibility for the success of the companies that their efforts might have even somewhat contaminated the experiment results. The project director in Athens, Georgia, for example, was so concerned about the project that at the beginning he threatened to terminate the experiment unless Plan Education Centers made certain revisions. He recommended additional teaching materials, enlisted consultants from the University of Georgia to assist the contractor, and saw to it that the latter hired more teaching staff.[2] As it turned out, this was one of the most successful sites in the experiment. Other project directors played a similar but lesser role, and in fact there was often tension between these people and the OEO staff who were less inclined to go out of their way to help the contractors because they felt it might bias the results of the experiment.

In chapter 2 it was mentioned that both national teacher organizations were opposed to performance contracting. This opposition was in some instances carried down to the local level. The companies were often hindered by the hostility of the regular teachers in the experimental schools. This was partly due to the inadequate attempts to enlist local teacher cooperation at the start of the experiment (a point discussed later) but it largely reflected more basic tensions. The regular teachers did not particularly enjoy competition, they were envious of teachers

1. This summary description is based on telephone interviews with the twenty project directors or their assistants.
2. Telephone interview with the Athens project director, J. C. Mullis.

either brought in from outside or hired locally at higher salaries by the companies, and they were upset by the scheduling disruptions caused by the presence of experimental classrooms in their schools. Even such seemingly reconcilable matters as the fact that teachers in the experiment often did not have cafeteria duty snowballed into large grievances. These problems, whether they could have been avoided or not, certainly did not make it any easier for the firms.

Launching the Experiment

Unfortunately the experiment did not get off to a very good start. Performance contracting became a hot educational issue in the early months of 1970, and in its haste to take advantage of this opportunity, OEO rushed precipitously into the planning of the experiment. Beginning with a visit to Texarkana in March 1970, the agency approved the experiment by April, advertised for contractors on April 27, and simultaneously sent requests for proposals to over twenty private companies. At about the same time it also awarded a contract for management support in the running of the experiment to Education Turnkey Systems, the firm that had handled the Texarkana arrangements. The extensive company selection process was completed within two months, and so was the process for selecting school districts. Most of the performance contracts between the companies, school districts, and OEO were signed by mid-July, when the agency also solicited proposals from about fifty testing and analysis companies. Battelle Memorial Institute was awarded this contract in August and was in the field doing the pretests two weeks later. Thus the experiment had actually begun by August 1970, barely six months after the OEO staff had first heard of Texarkana.

Although the original model for performance contracting, the Dorsett Educational Systems program in Texarkana, had started with about the same time span for planning, and although the six private firms had advertised their teaching experience while winning the bids from OEO, most of them were not well prepared to begin teaching in three separate sites and eighteen different schools just two months after they received the OEO bids in June. They were hard pressed even to hire enough local teachers to staff their programs, let alone solicit the advice and support of local teachers and other school officials. When equipment and instructional materials necessary for their teaching programs did not arrive in time, programs had to be hastily revised and other materials used.

The school districts encountered similar problems. School officials were asked to do a considerable amount of preparatory work. They had to assemble lists of students who might take part, secure the cooperation of teachers and principals in the schools chosen for the experiment, and provide a project director and two aides. For the most part, the districts managed to complete these tasks by the fall, but they could do little to prepare either teachers or principals in participating schools, most of whom did not even find out about the project until they returned from their summer vacations.[3]

These start-up problems were especially bad in the sites using teacher incentives. OEO's decision to include two sites in the experiment where incentive contracts were to be signed directly with the local teacher organizations was not made until the summer before the experiment was to begin. This meant little choice—in fact, no choice—of school district. Only two submitted formal proposals—Mesa, Arizona, and Stockton, California—and they were both included in the experiment. Because of this late start, both sites were still securing formal approvals from teacher organizations, state and local boards of education, governors, and community groups until the fall; both sites were still negotiating their incentive contracts until November; and Mesa did not even receive the advance on its incentive payments until almost Christmas.[4]

A final set of problems involved the pretesting of students. Battelle Institute was not awarded a contract until just before it was to begin testing almost 30,000 children. It had had no experience in organizing such large-scale testing programs and little time to schedule the exams, arrange for rooms, and train test administrators. As a consequence, testing conditions for the pretest were poor in many sites, in both experimental and control classrooms. In its *Report on Pretesting,* Battelle notes many instances of lack of discipline, overcrowded conditions, and excessively hot classrooms, and isolated instances of minor student riots and even a fire drill in the middle of a test period. In a few cases the

---

3. Telephone interviews with project directors.

4. Douglas P. Barnard and others, "Project Directors' Perception of 'Incentives Only' Project," in U.S. Office of Economic Opportunity, Office of Planning, Research, and Evaluation, *A Demonstration of Incentives in Education,* OEO Pamphlet 3400-7 (1972).

problems were so severe that the students were retested a few weeks later.[5]

Obtaining the Consent of Parents

One area little noticed at the time but in which the experiment established a fairly good record was obtaining the consent of the parents of students in the experimental group. This issue—and the related larger question of the ethics of social experimentation—received some prominence in 1973 as a result of some very questionable practices in certain public health experiments.

Ethical issues arise in an experiment because the sponsoring agency is not trying to institute the best policy, but rather varying treatments in a supposedly scientific way so as to generate information to be of practical use later. In this case, for example, OEO was asking school districts to sign up with performance contracting companies for one year, even though the agency had not yet made up its mind about performance contracting as a policy to be adopted on a wider basis. Since the experimental treatment would have uncertain effects—it could make students better off academically, but it could also make them worse off— there is a possible moral problem involved.

The tradition in the early social experiments, as in the fields of medicine and psychology, which have grappled with this issue for a much longer time, is to do the experiment anyway as long as the subjects give their consent under conditions that imply reasonable knowledge of what it is all about, and as long as there is no chance of very great harm to the human subjects.[6] The "very great harm" clause is usually interpreted to apply to medical disasters or death and is probably not relevant in the case of an education experiment lasting for just one year. But the "informed consent" clause becomes much more difficult to interpret in

5. Criticism of the Battelle testing operation can be found in the "Project Managers' Statement," in U.S. Office of Economic Opportunity, Office of Planning, Research, and Evaluation, *An Experiment in Performance Contracting*, OEO Pamphlet 3400-6 (1972), pp. 217–18. The Battelle test report is in Battelle Columbus Laboratories, *Report on Pretesting for the Office of Economic Opportunity Performance Incentive Experiment in Education* (Columbus, Ohio: Battelle Memorial Institute, 1971).

6. These points are covered in a Brookings research study on the ethics of social experimentation supervised by Alice M. Rivlin and P. Michael Timpane.

education experiments because it is very difficult to define the appropriate consenting unit.

One interpretation is that the OEO performance contracting project was an experiment with school districts, not students, and that it is sufficient to obtain only the consent of the policymaking body for the school district. Since OEO had already obtained this consent—each district volunteered for the experiment—this interpretation would suggest that it was unnecessary to go further. A second, more conservative interpretation holds that for a school board to sign up for a national experiment under which private firms will actually teach students in the public schools goes beyond what it could approve under its normal policymaking authority. In this case the school district should therefore have gained the consent of the subjects involved. That would mean the parents in this experiment, since all students were under fifteen. The matter was never considered very carefully, except possibly in internal deliberations within the general counsel's office at OEO, but the latter interpretation seems to have been followed in most districts.[7]

Miscellaneous Problems

There were also a few sites where extraordinary difficulties occurred, much beyond anything that might have been anticipated beforehand and sometimes so serious as to make the test results next to meaningless. The worst was the Bronx. In the late sixties the New York City school system had moved toward a decentralized, community-controlled system that had antagonized its strong local teachers' union, the United Federation of Teachers. This union, a chapter of the American Federation of Teachers, was as opposed as its parent to performance contracting, and its president, Albert Shanker, announced on the radio that he believed the OEO Bronx program to be illegal and threatened action to prevent its continuation.[8] The teachers in the experimental schools took

7. Several OEO personnel involved in the experiment volunteered this information. The only documentation found on the issue implies that there were several sites where parental consent was not solicited. See Education Turnkey Systems, *Final Report to OEO: Performance Incentive Remedial Education Experiment,* Final Report to the Office of Economic Opportunity, BOO-5114 (Washington, D.C.: Education Turnkey Systems, Inc., 1971), pp. 197–98.

8. Reported in "Shanker Hits OEO Schools," *New York News,* September 21, 1970.

this cue and were continually at loggerheads with the contractor, Learning Foundations. There were reports that they threw some of the Learning Foundations equipment out of second-story windows and told students to throw away their parent questionnaires. Discipline in the junior high schools involved in the experiment became so bad at one point early in the fall that all testing and instruction were halted and a full-time policeman had to be stationed in one of them. Instruction could only be resumed when the president of Learning Foundations, Fran Tarkenton, at that time also quarterback of the New York Giants football team, was able to rally community support around the project. Even so, records from the project are very incomplete. The tests at the end of the school year were given in a ballroom a few blocks from the school and a new form of attrition was introduced as students walked from the school to the testing room. Moreover, some of the ninth grade control students were not post-tested because the school principal assigned Battelle a testing date that was after the school year was over, the parent questionnaires and student information cards were never filled out, and the project director kept very poor records of who was and who was not in the program.[9] Fortunately, this experience was out of the ordinary.

The situation in Hartford and Philadelphia was almost as disorganized. According to an April 1971 OEO memo, a strike closed both the experimental and control schools for thirteen days in Hartford, and the contractor claimed that another fourteen days had been lost because of classroom disruptions. Furthermore, there were reports that about seventy-five of the 300 elementary students in the experimental group did not start the program until late October, which was more than a month after the other students. In Philadelphia, there was a short school strike, much of the teaching equipment was vandalized, and the contractor's junior high school staff walked off the job to protest the firing of one person. There was also considerable conflict between the contractor's staff and school personnel.

There were disruptions in a few other sites. In Taft, Texas, a number of Chicano parents pulled their children out of a ninth grade class because there were only Chicanos in the class. Taft also had a hurricane, which blew the roof off one of the schools at the beginning of the school

9. This information comes mainly from interviews with Jeffry Schiller, director of the OEO Experimental Research Division at the time of the experiment, and Charles Stalford, the OEO project manager.

year. The experiment in Wichita began in confusion because the district was then redrawing school zone lines to correspond with a court integration ruling.

How SERIOUS THESE FIELD PROBLEMS were and the degree to which they might have obscured the results of the experiment cannot be precisely analyzed. While in a few sites the results are no doubt useless, in most sites the experiment proceeded reasonably smoothly, indicating that it is at least possible to operate field experiments such as this OEO project. But, given the enormous difficulties of planning and implementation, it is still difficult to know how much credence to place in the results. The obvious point is that experiments can get into trouble, as this one did, if there is too little time to plan, and too little effort is made to gain the cooperation and support of the local personnel who are ultimately responsible for the successful operation of the project.

4. The Results

The key question to be decided by the experiment was whether or not the private companies did in fact outperform the public schools in the control group. To find the answer, the overall test scores of the experimental and control groups are first compared and then disaggregated in various ways: by grade and subject, by components of the achievement tests, by the scholastic deficiencies of students, and by individual sites. The extent to which attrition, measurement error, testing problems, or other types of bias might contaminate the results is also discussed. Finally, by examining the daily attendance records of students in the experimental and control groups and the reports from project directors in the field, an attempt is made to see what other factors, if any, might suggest a different interpretation of the experiment's results.

Interpreting Test Results

There are three important statistical problems that might cloud the meaning of the results. The first—a common problem in any experiment such as this—is attrition. The experiment was conducted with academically underprivileged students attending academically underprivileged schools. Typically this is a very mobile student population, and the ones involved in the performance contracting project were no exception. Of the initial sample of 24,000 students in the control and experimental groups, only 19,400—81 percent—remained in the program for the full school year. And, owing to the inevitable absences on test day, the fact that some students could not complete the tests, and the fact that in one site, the Bronx, some of the tests were not given because of scheduling errors, only 14,650 students—61 percent of the initial sample—completed the full set of evaluation tests at the beginning and end of the experiment.

Large attrition in and of itself would not necessarily bias the results, but it could if it were much larger in either the experimental or the control group. If it were larger, and if the students who failed to complete all tests differed in some systematic way from those who took all tests, a comparison of the test scores of those who remained could be misleading. In this experiment, if the least promising students were the ones who, for one reason or another, did not take all tests, and if there were more of these dropouts in the control group, a simple comparison of average gains would be biased against students in the experimental group.

To determine if this is a serious problem, Table 4-1 presents data

Table 4-1. Attrition and Test Data for Experimental and Control Groups, by Grade, 1970–71 School Year

Student and test items by group	Grade						All grades
	1	2	3	7	8	9	
1. *Number of students in initial sample*							
Experimental	2,000	2,000	2,000	2,000	2,000	2,000	12,000
Control	2,000	2,000	2,000	2,000	2,000	2,000	12,000
2. *Number of students remaining in program entire year*							
Experimental	1,653	1,709	1,727	1,631	1,676	1,578	9,974
Control	1,526	1,626	1,553	1,612	1,557	1,551	9,425
3. *Percentage of initial sample remaining entire year*							
Experimental	83	85	86	82	84	79	83
Control	76	81	78	81	78	78	79
4. *Number of students who took pre- and post-tests*							
Experimental	1,196	1,377	1,400	1,289	1,241	1,202	7,705
Control	1,166	1,161	1,202	1,185	1,165	1,061	6,940
5. *Percentage of full-year students who took pre- and post-tests*							
Experimental	72	81	81	79	74	76	77
Control	76	71	77	74	75	68	74
6. *Mean pretest*[a] *scores in reading*							
Experimental	[b]	1.5	2.2	4.5	4.8	5.6	...
Control	[b]	1.6	2.3	5.0	5.6	6.4	...
7. *Mean pretest*[a] *scores in mathematics*							
Experimental	[b]	1.4	2.2	4.7	5.4	6.0	...
Control	[b]	1.4	2.3	4.9	5.9	6.6	...

Source: Compiled from test data provided by Battelle Columbus Laboratories on the Office of Economic Opportunity experiment in educational performance contracting, 1970–71 school year.

n.a. Not available.

a. In-grade equivalent units on the 1970 version of the Metropolitan Achievement Test Series. See Jeffry S. Schiller and Ellen P. Murdoch, "Implications of Using Standardized Tests in Performance Contracting," in Office of Economic Opportunity, Office of Planning, Research, and Evaluation, *An Experiment in Performance Contracting*, OEO Pamphlet 3400-6 (1972), pp. 51–65, for further details.

b. In grade 1, the California Achievement Test, which has no grade equivalent conversion, was used for the pretest.

on the number of students participating at various stages in the experiment. The first part of the table (rows 1 to 4) disaggregates attrition by experimental status and according to whether students dropped out during the year or simply did not complete all tests. There are good reasons for these figures to show a higher proportion of dropouts in the control sample, as indeed they do in row 3. This is because both the experimental and control samples were selected initially from school records for the previous year, and when students moved out of the district before the school year began the experimental sample was replenished from the replacement group whereas the control sample was not.

But there is no obvious reason for differences in the proportion of full-year students who completed all evaluation tests (given in row 5). The slight differences reported suggest that disproportionate attrition could be responsible for a small bias against the students in the experiment, especially if the experiment was itself responsible for the lower attrition in that group.[1]

A second problem stems from the procedures used to select schools and students. These procedures (discussed in chapter 2) implied that participating students generally ranked lower academically than their counterparts in the control group at the start of the experiment, by amounts (in rows 6 and 7 of Table 4-1) that are negligible in lower grades but somewhat more noticeable in the upper grades. These initial differences could lead to a bias in the comparison of mean gains, because student gains might depend systematically on initial test scores. But since the way in which average gains depend on pretest scores can be measured, adjustment factors can be constructed to apply to the observed mean gain differences to give unbiased results. These adjustment factors, derived in an earlier OEO report, are of almost no importance in the overall results for upper grades, but of somewhat more importance in certain individual sites where initial differences are larger.[2]

1. A close examination of the grade-by-grade percentages can better pinpoint possible bias. In the first grade the control percentage taking the tests is higher than the experimental percentage because first grade evaluation tests were not given to participating students in the Bronx; and the much higher experimental percentage in the ninth grade is because tests were not given to the Bronx students in the control group. Thus the bias, if present, should exist in the results for only the second, third, and seventh grades.

2. See Irwin Garfinkel and Edward M. Gramlich, "A Statistical Analysis of the OEO Experiment in Educational Performance Contracting," *Journal of Human Resources,* vol. 8 (Summer 1973), pp. 275–305; also published in Office of Economic Opportunity, Office of Planning, Research, and Evaluation, *An Experiment*

A final problem, which is more serious because it is harder to correct, concerns testing problems in individual sites. If testing measurement errors are random and generally average out for groups of students, as in the above case, there are statistical procedures for adjusting gains to determine the true differences between the experimental and control groups. But if the disturbances are common to a whole group of students, such as poor testing conditions affecting an entire site, then it becomes much more difficult to construct appropriate adjustments for these particular sites.

Since the reports of test monitors indicate that sitewide testing problems did exist in certain locations, especially during the pretests, it is necessary to correct for such disturbances.[3] For the control groups this could be done by comparing the experimental gains in individual sites with control gains across the entire experiment, and for the experimental groups by comparing gains on the evaluation and payments tests. However, neither procedure is an infallible substitute for good testing conditions. For this reason, along with the fact that the sample of students is much smaller in each individual site, site comparisons are a good deal less reliable than the overall results across all twenty sites.

Overall Results

The Metropolitan Achievement Tests used in evaluating the performance contractors in five of the six grades have several components. In the elementary grades the achievement tests consist of two reading components—reading and word knowledge—three mathematics components—computation, concepts, and problems—and components for word analysis and spelling that are not part of either the reading or mathematics score. In the upper grades the reading and mathematics components are the same as in the elementary tests, but there are also additional subtests for language, spelling, science, and social studies. The peripheral subjects such as science and social studies were not taught by

---

in *Performance Contracting*, OEO Pamphlet 3400-6 (1972), pp. 1–50. This article also discusses why multiple regression methods of analyzing the data also give biased results because of measurement error in pretest scores.

3. Battelle Columbus Laboratories, *Final Report on the Office of Economic Opportunity Experiment in Educational Performance Contracting* (Columbus, Ohio: Battelle Memorial Institute, 1972), pp. 53–62.

Table 4-2. Differences in Gain between Experimental and Control Groups, by Grade and Test Subcomponent, 1970–71 School Year[a]

Raw score points

Subcomponents	Grade[b]				
	2	3	7	8	9
Reading	−0.6	1.7	1.0	−0.7	0.8
Word knowledge	0.2	0.7	0.6	−0.5	0.2
Reading	−0.8	1.0	0.4	−0.2	0.6
Mathematics	0.5	0.0	−1.1	−2.3	0.2
Computation	0.2	−0.2	0.5	−0.5	0.5
Concepts	0.3	−0.2	−0.6	−0.9	0.0
Problems	n.a.	0.4	−1.0	−0.9	−0.3
Other	−0.3	−0.1	−3.7	−1.2	−9.0
Word analysis	−0.3	−0.1	n.a.	n.a.	n.a.
Spelling	n.a.	n.a.	−0.9	0.0	−0.8
Language	n.a.	n.a.	−1.3	0.8	−2.1
Science	n.a.	n.a.	−0.2	−1.1	−2.4
Social studies	n.a.	n.a.	−1.3	−0.9	−3.7

Source: Same as Table 4-1.

n.a. Not available. There is no subtest for this topic in that grade.

a. Mean gain of students in experimental group less mean gain of students in control group.

b. Since different tests were used for the first grade pre- and post-tests, the subcomponents for these scores are not available.

the contractors, but since the tests came as a package these components were given to all students anyway, with the thought that if the contractors helped students to read better, the students might also do better in social studies and other subjects.

Table 4-2 presents the differences in mean gains on these achievement test subcomponents between experimental and control groups, aggregated across all sites for the entire sample of 14,650 students who were at school for the full year and took all the tests (roughly 2,900 in each grade). Since a different test series was used for the first grade pretests and post-tests, these scores could not be disaggregated by component.

The table indicates several things. First, the differences between experimental and control gains in reading and mathematics, the subjects actually taught in the experiment, are quite small in almost every case. The reading results suggest that the participating students did slightly better, the mathematics results slightly worse, but both margins are small. The largest difference, −2.3 raw score points in eighth grade mathematics, converts to only about 0.2 of a grade equivalent unit.

A second feature is that just as the total mean gain differences for reading and mathematics are small, so are the differences on each sub-test in both subjects. There seems to be no obvious tendency for the contractors to do relatively better in, say, word knowledge than in reading, or in mathematical computation than in mathematical concepts.

But the table does show one interesting set of differences. When the performance of students in the experimental and control groups is compared in subjects not taught by the contractors—spelling, language, science, and social studies—students in the control group generally did better. With the lone exception of eighth grade language, participating students did the same or worse in every subcomponent of every test—sometimes, as in ninth grade, by quite large amounts. Since students in the experiment were presumably learning these subjects in their normal classrooms—which were presumably similar to the classrooms attended by students in the control schools—it is difficult to say what these differences indicate. One interpretation is that the disruption of going to special classrooms in the school put the students in the experiment behind in other subjects, possibly because with imperfect school scheduling they actually missed some instruction. Another is that after the individualized and incentive-based learning in the contractors' classrooms, the students in the experimental group had more trouble with the traditional techniques generally used in classrooms where other subjects were taught. A third is that the measured experimental achievement gains in reading and mathematics, even though no higher than for students in the control group, were for some reason higher than the true gains.[4] Without further evidence one can merely wonder what were the prevailing factors.

But whatever the case, the experiment was designed to analyze relative gains in reading and mathematics. The basic comparison of these gains is presented in Table 4-3. Row 1 shows the mean gain differences in reading and mathematics for the six grades: 1, 2, 3, 7, 8, and 9. The figures in row 2 are adjusted to take into account the fact that the experimental students belonged to a somewhat lower-ranking population than the control students. Since in most cases achievement gains are found to be positively related to initial test scores, which are always higher for students in the control schools, the adjustments generally benefit the experimental students (which is to say that the unadjusted mean gain differences are slightly biased against these students in the experiment). The

---

4. See p. 43, note 8, for another indication that this may be true.

Table 4-3. Differences in Gain between Experimental and Control Groups, by Grade and Subject, 1970–71 School Year[a]

	Grade											
	1		2		3		7		8		9	
Difference item	Reading	Mathe-matics	Reading	Mathe-matics	Reading	Mathe-matics	Reading	Mathe-matics	Reading	Mathe-matics	Reading	Mathe-matics
1. Mean gain differences, in raw score points	0.8	0.0	−0.6	0.5	1.7[b]	0.0	1.0[b]	−1.1[b]	−0.7	−2.3[b]	0.8	0.2
2. Adjustment for differential in starting points, in raw score points[c]	−0.6	−0.8	1.3	−0.1	2.2	0.5	0.8	1.0	1.1	1.0	0.5	0.9
3. Adjusted mean gain differences, in raw score points (row 1 + row 2)	0.2	−0.8	0.7	0.4	3.9[b]	0.5	1.8[b]	−0.1	0.4	−1.3[b]	1.3[b]	1.1[b]
4. Adjusted mean gain differences, in grade equivalent units	0.0	0.0	0.1	0.0	0.1	0.0	0.2	0.0	0.0	−0.1	0.1	0.1
5. Adjusted gain difference at bottom of distribution in grade equivalent units[d]	0.1	0.1	0.0	0.0	0.1	0.0	0.3	0.2	0.1	0.2	0.1	0.3
6. Adjusted gain difference for students at top of distribution, in grade equivalent units[d]	−0.1	−0.2	0.1	0.0	0.1	0.0	0.1	−0.2	0.0	−0.5	0.1	−0.1

Source: Same as Table 4.1.

a. Mean gain of students in experimental group less mean gain of students in control group.

b. Indicates statistical significance at 0.05 level.

c. Adjustments were made through a procedure described in Irwin Garfinkel and Edward M. Gramlich, "A Statistical Analysis of the OEO Experiment in Educational Performance Contracting," cited in text, pages 34–35, note 2.

d. For students two standard deviations below and above the average, using a regression procedure described in Garfinkel and Gramlich, "A Statistical Analysis of the OEO Experiment."

adjusted mean gain differences in row 3 are probably the best measures of the relative performance of the experimental and control groups. They show statistically significant experimental gains four times, one statistically significant experimental loss, and very small gains or losses in the other seven cases. In terms of the grade equivalent conversions, shown in row 4, there is only one case, seventh grade reading, where students in the experiment gained as much as 0.2 grade equivalent unit more than the other students, four cases of 0.1 grade equivalent gain, and one case, eighth grade mathematics, of a 0.1 grade equivalent loss. Again, students in the experimental classes seemed to have fared slightly better than the ones in traditional classes in reading, but this time about the same in mathematics.

The adjusted experimental gains shown in row 4, averaging about 0.04 of a grade equivalent unit—7 percent more gain than students in the control group—can be given different interpretations. The gains were much less than initially expected by almost everybody involved in the experiment—the contractors, the school district personnel, and OEO. This explains why the immediate reaction was disappointment, and why the popular impression of performance contracting was that the firms had failed. At the same time, it can be argued that while the relative gains are far less than needed for students in the experiment to keep up with the average students, the overall results are positive. If the experimental classes had continued, they would have eliminated roughly one-tenth of the achievement deficit of underprivileged students. When account is taken of all the start-up difficulties experienced by the contractors, the firms' performance may actually have been as good as anybody had a right to expect. Thus, just as OEO's expectation of great success led to certain problems in the design of the experiment, it also may have led to an overly pessimistic initial reporting of the results.

One explanation for the relatively small comparative gains, advanced by the General Accounting Office among others, is that the control schools and their teachers may have tried harder during the year because they felt threatened by performance contracting.[5] There was outright teacher hostility to the experiment in several sites: sufficiently serious in two sites for the OEO to abandon the incentive contracts and recompute payments on a cost-plus basis (see chapter 5). This hostility could also have led the

5. *Evaluation of the Office of Economic Opportunity's Performance Contracting Experiment,* Report to the Congress by the Comptroller General of the United States, B-130515 (1973), p. 19.

Table 4-4. Pretest and Post-Test Scores of Students in the Experimental Group, and Gains, by Grade and Subject, 1970–71 School Year

Grade equivalent units

		Grade										
	1		2		3		7		8		9	
Item	Reading	Mathematics	Reading	Mathematics	Reading	Mathematics	Reading	Mathematics	Reading	Mathematics	Reading	Mathematics
1. Pretest score	n.a.	n.a.	1.5	1.4	2.2	2.2	4.5	4.7	4.8	5.4	5.6	6.0
2. Post-test score	1.0	1.3	1.9	1.9	2.5	2.6	4.9	5.3	5.7	6.2	6.4	6.8
3. Gain	n.a.	n.a.	0.4	0.5	0.3	0.4	0.4	0.6	0.9	0.8	0.8	0.8
4. Grade behind at start[a]	n.a.	n.a.	0.5	0.6	0.8	0.8	2.5	2.3	3.2	2.6	3.4	3.0
5. Grade behind at end[b]	0.9	0.6	1.0	1.0	1.4	1.3	3.0	2.6	3.2	2.7	3.5	3.1

Source: Same as Table 4-1.
n.a. Not available. See Table 4-1, note b.
a. For any grade subtract the pretest mean from the grade number.
b. For any grade subtract the post-test mean from the next highest grade number less 0.1.

control schools to spend more time in reading and mathematics instruction than usual, or to try to stimulate students in the control group to perform unusually well in other ways. If such were the case, the observed gains of both the experimental and control groups would also be abnormally high—the performance contractors would not do better than the control schools during this experiment, but better than control schools normally do.

Table 4-4 indicates that there does not appear to be much basis for this contention. It gives the absolute grade equivalent gains broken down by grade and subject, for the 7,700 students in the experiment who participated for the full year and who took all the tests. The absolute experimental gains in row 3 are always less than a grade equivalent unit (the amount a normal student would gain), in the lower grades significantly less. The average experimental gain of 0.6 grade equivalent unit is about the same as students in both the experimental and control groups would have gained in normal circumstances in order to start at the beginning of the school year as far behind average grade levels as they did. Thus, although the control schools may have tried to do better during the experiment, the students' performance suggests that neither they nor the performance contractors seem to have actually done much better. The marginal gains made by the performance contracting students fell well short of what would be required to eliminate the achievement deficiencies of these students.[6]

A final possibility indicated by the overall results is that performance contracting might have differentially affected students at different points in the pretest distribution. The companies were advertising teaching programs for disadvantaged students, and they may very well have fared better with students far behind the norms and worse with students relatively close to the norms.

This possibility was investigated using a regression test designed to determine whether the effect of the experiment was greater or less on

6. This test also indicates that the widely feared Hawthorne effect—the possibility that students in the experiment would do better simply because they felt they were being attended to—was probably not a significant problem. (The term Hawthorne effect originated from a study of the effect of monotony on workers, made at the Hawthorne Works of the Western Electric Company in Chicago between 1927 and 1932. It was found that when management paid attention—no matter what kind—to workers, output increased. For example, decreasing illumination, as well as increasing it, caused output to rise. The same phenomenon has been observed in other social experiments.)

Table 4-5. Grade Equivalent Gains of Experimental over Control Groups, by Site, Contractor, Grade, and Subject, 1970–71 School Year

Grade equivalent units

Site and contractor	Grade 1 Reading	Grade 1 Mathematics	Grade 2 Reading	Grade 2 Mathematics	Grade 3 Reading	Grade 3 Mathematics	Grade 7 Reading	Grade 7 Mathematics	Grade 8 Reading	Grade 8 Mathematics	Grade 9 Reading	Grade 9 Mathematics	All grades
Learning Foundations													
Bronx, New York	n.a.	n.a.	0.2[a]	-0.2	-0.1	-0.2[a]	0.2	0.2[a]	-0.3	-0.4	n.a.	n.a.	-0.08
Jacksonville, Florida	0.7[a]	0.7[a]	0.0	0.4	0.2	0.2	-0.2	0.0	0.2	0.0	0.3	0.0	0.21
Hammond, Indiana	-0.5[a]	0.0	0.0[b]	0.0[b]	0.0	0.0	0.0	0.3	0.0	0.0	0.2	0.1	0.01
Westinghouse Learning Corporation													
Philadelphia, Pennsylvania	-0.7[a]	-0.9	-0.1[b]	-0.3	0.0	0.0	-0.2	0.0	-0.7[a]	0.4	-0.5	-0.4	-0.28
Fresno, California	0.0[c]	-0.7	0.0	-0.2	0.0	-0.1	0.4	-0.4[a]	-0.2	-0.1	0.6	0.4	-0.02
Las Vegas, Nevada	0.0	-0.9	-0.3	-0.2[b]	-0.2	-0.5[a]	0.2	-0.3	0.2	-0.2	0.7	0.2	-0.11
Quality Educational Development Corporation													
Dallas, Texas	0.4	0.4	0.1[c]	0.1	0.1	0.6[a]	0.5[a]	-0.2	0.7[a]	0.9	0.0	0.0	0.30
Anchorage, Alaska	0.1[c]	0.4[a]	0.2	0.3	0.2	0.2	0.0	0.4[a]	1.1	-0.2	0.5[a, b]	1.0	0.35
Rockland, Maine	-0.1	0.0	0.2	0.2	0.4[a]	0.4[a]	0.0[b]	0.1	0.4	0.1	0.7[a]	1.1[a]	0.29
Alpha Learning Systems													
Grand Rapids, Michigan	0.3	-0.3	0.1[b]	-0.1	0.0	-0.1	0.1	-0.2	0.9	-0.6[a]	0.5	0.0	0.05
Hartford, Connecticut	-0.2	-0.6[a]	0.0[b]	0.0	0.2	-0.1	0.0	0.0	-0.2	-0.2	0.1	0.5	-0.04
Taft, Texas	0.0	-0.1[d]	0.0	0.1[b]	0.0	0.4[a]	0.1	0.1	0.1	0.3	1.1[a]	0.2	0.19
Singer/Graflex													
Seattle, Washington	-0.8[a]	-0.3	0.0	-0.2	0.1	0.0	0.1	-0.5	-0.9[a]	-1.4	-0.1	-0.9[a]	-0.41
Portland, Maine	-0.4	-0.6	0.0	-0.2	0.0[d]	-0.1	0.3	0.3	0.0	-0.2	-0.2	-0.5[a]	-0.13
McComb, Mississippi	0.4	1.0	0.0	0.0	0.1[d]	-0.1[d]	0.2	0.0	-0.1	-0.2	0.2	0.0	0.12
Plan Education Centers													
Wichita, Kansas	-0.8	-0.1	0.2	0.1	0.2	0.1[b]	0.0	0.0	0.0	0.1	0.0	0.0	-0.02
Athens, Georgia	0.0	0.2	0.0	0.0	0.2	0.3	0.4[a]	0.5	-0.1	-0.2	0.4	0.6	0.19
Selmer, Tennessee	0.9	0.2	0.0	0.1	0.5	0.5	0.0	0.0	0.1	0.4[a]	0.6[a]	-0.2	0.26
Local teacher organization[e]													
Stockton, California	0.7[a]	0.2	0.2	0.5[b]	0.0	0.0	0.0	0.1	-0.3	0.2	-0.6[a]	0.0	0.12
Mesa, Arizona	0.1	-0.1[d]	0.2	0.5[a]	-0.2	-0.2[c]	0.0	-0.1	0.4	0.0	-0.2	0.6	0.03
Average	0.01	-0.08	0.05	0.04	0.08	0.06	0.10	0.02	0.06	-0.06	0.23	0.13	0.05

Source: Same as Table 4-1.
n.a. Not available. Tests were not given because of scheduling errors.
a. A significant difference (at the 95 percent confidence level) in the adjusted mean gain difference is eliminated by pooling control students.
b. Gains by the experimental group on the payments tests are significantly higher than gains on evaluation tests.
c. An insignificant difference in the adjusted mean gain difference becomes significantly negative when control students are pooled.
d. An insignificant difference in the adjusted mean gain difference becomes significantly positive when control students are pooled.
e. The experiment involved incentive payment for local teachers.

students with low pretest scores. The test, described in detail in a 1971 OEO report,[7] indicates that students in the experiment with low pretest scores did fare somewhat better than participating students with high scores in about half of the twelve grade-subject cases. But again, the relative difference in performance is only large in one case, eighth grade mathematics, as shown in rows 5 and 6 of Table 4-3.

Results for Individual Sites

It is also possible to examine results on a site-by-site basis. These comparisons are less reliable than the overall comparisons because there are sites with smaller samples than others and sites with testing problems, but they may be more relevant—especially if performance contracting worked particularly well in certain types of situations and with certain companies.

Table 4-5 compares the individual sites for each of the six grades. It presents average differences in gains between the experimental and control groups in grade equivalent units, adjusted for initial pretest differences shown in Table 4-3, row 4. Then, to take large gains or losses due to testing problems into account, there are two separate adjustments. For control group testing problems in individual sites, experimental gains are compared with the adjusted gains for control groups across all sites (Table 4-5, notes a, c, and d). Experimental site testing problems could not be discerned from such a procedure because it would be impossible to tell whether individual site abnormalities reflected the experimental program or not. Therefore evaluation test gains were compared with gains of the same students on the payments tests (Table 4-5, note b).[8]

7. See Garfinkel and Gramlich, "A Statistical Analysis of the OEO Experiment."

8. For some mysterious reason, the measured gains of experimental students on the payments tests (which students in the control groups did not take) were lower than on the evaluation tests over 70 percent of the time. Thus the table only indicates cases where gains in payments tests are higher than those in the evaluation tests, and hence where there is suspicion that evaluation test gains are understated.

The fact that evaluation test gains generally were greater than payments test gains is the other indication, referred to above, that the evaluation tests for reading and mathematics may be catching students in the experiment at their atypical best.

Table 4-6. Regressions Explaining the Differences in Individual Site Results, by Grade, Contractor, Region, and Other Characteristics, 1970–71 School Year[a]

	Dependent variable		
	Mean difference in raw score points[b]		*Mean difference between control and experimental groups in percentage of absent students*[c]
Independent variable	*Between experimental and control groups* (1)	*Between experimental and pooled control groups* (2)	(3)
Constant	−2.36 (−3.3)	−0.51 (−1.3)	0.44 (1.3)
Grade 3	2.18 (2.5)	...	...
Grade 9	1.85 (2.1)	...	...
Learning Foundations	...	...	−3.20 (−3.4)
Westinghouse Learning Corporation	−1.80 (−1.9)	...	...
Quality Educational Development Corporation	6.58 (6.2)	2.23 (2.7)	...
Singer/Graflex	...	...	−3.68 (−5.6)
Low instructional cost	...	...	−0.60 (−0.9)
Lost instructional time	...	...	3.35 (3.6)
Large city[d]	...	...	2.68 (4.0)
Medium-sized city[d]	1.88 (2.2)	...	...
City with large Chicano population	4.02 (2.6)	3.17 (2.4)	...
Northeast region	...	...	−2.79 (−3.3)
Southeast region	5.65 (4.7)	3.59 (3.7)	...
North Central region	...	1.63 (1.7)	...
South Central region	5.11 (4.2)	4.63 (4.7)	...
R^2	0.275	0.130	0.360
Standard error	4.89	4.36	2.15

There are very few large winners and losers in these individual site comparisons. The last column indicates that in no site are the overall average experimental gains as much as 0.5 grade equivalent unit more or less than those of the control groups. Of the total number of 236 average differences in gains, there are only twenty-seven experimental groups gaining as much as 0.5 (Table 4-5). Moreover, if the control groups are pooled, twelve of the twenty-seven experimental "successes" and eleven of the nineteen "failures" disappear (offset by only a small number of insignificant differences that are created by the pooling). Nor do the payments tests provide many examples of experimental success not recorded because of site testing problems with the participating students. Thus these numbers provide little basis for believing that the overall results are masking offsetting successes and failures—there are some, but relatively few.

With so many individual site comparisons, it is difficult to discern more subtle patterns in the results by simply using averages. It is difficult to tell, for instance, how grade, subject, time spent, cost, company, region, size of district, racial composition, or any other feature might have influenced the test score results. A better means of conducting such tests is through multiple regression analysis (Table 4-6). Regressions were estimated where the dependent variable is either the raw score equivalent of the grade equivalent gains given in Table 4-5 or the analogous data (not shown in Table 4-5) based on pooled control groups. The independent variables in these regressions are a set of dummy variables (1 if category X, otherwise 0) referring to the above characteristics that might have affected student achievement. The regression coefficients and their statistical significance levels then indicate whether the individual site results bear any systematic relationship to these categories or are simply randomly distributed. The coefficients for these two regressions, with those variables not having statistically significant coefficients deleted, are given in the first two columns of Table 4-6.

Source: Regressions based on test data cited in Table 4-1.

a. All variables have been tested through the use of dummies. Insignificant variables are omitted from the final regressions. The numbers in parentheses are *t*-ratios.

b. Generally one raw score point translates to about 0.067 of a grade equivalent gain in the lower grades and 0.10 in the upper grades. There were 236 observations.

c. A positive coefficient means that this category was responsible for better attendance among the experimental students than among the control students, a negative coefficient the opposite relationship. There were 86 observations.

d. A large city has a population of over 1,000,000; a medium-sized city has a population of 500,000 to 1,000,000.

The regression coefficients imply the following:

1. There is no apparent statistical difference between test performance in reading and mathematics.

2. There are few grade differences, with the site-by-site comparisons showing the companies to be slightly better in grades 3 and 9. When the control groups are pooled there are no significant differences.

3. For companies, Quality Educational Development Corporation was more successful than the others in both comparisons, by amounts that could be educationally significant (from two to seven raw score points above the control groups). The first regression indicates that Westinghouse Learning Corporation was less successful by a somewhat smaller amount. The other firms and the local teacher organizations did about the same as the control groups.

4. Neither lost instructional time (due to unanticipated closing of school, short class hours, assemblies, or fire drills) nor cost differences between experimental and control students have any apparent effect on the pattern of test score results.[9]

5. The individual comparisons suggest that performance contracting works slightly better in medium-sized cities (with a population of between 500,000 to 1,000,000) than in other types of districts.

6. Both regressions suggest that performance contracting works slightly better in sites with a large Chicano population.

7. Both regressions suggest greater success for performance contracting in the Southeast and South Central regions, and the second regression also suggests a marginally better impact in the North Central region.

8. Although there are from four to seven statistically significant independent variables in the two regressions, the low R^2s indicate that there is a large random component in the test score results. Pooling the con-

9. One of the initial goals of the project, progressively abandoned as it ran its course, was to see if performance contracting companies could teach more cheaply than the control schools. Cost data were collected for ten sites by Education Turnkey Systems; they are presented in Charles B. Stalford, "Analysis of Program Cost," in OEO Pamphlet 3400-6, and criticized sharply in the "Contractors' Statement," same volume. These cost data show that on an overall basis performance contracting is not cheaper, indeed it is a little more expensive than the traditional programs. In the regression analysis we tried to probe the question of cost effectiveness more deeply by including dummies according to whether the site-grade-subject experimental costs were higher, lower, or the same as control school costs. These variables did not increase the explanatory power of either test score equation, though there was some slight effect on average daily attendance, see below.

trol groups (column 2) reduces the absolute importance of this random residual somewhat (as measured by the slight decline in the standard error), but it also reduces the R^2 because the variance of the dependent variable has been reduced even more.

Other Indications of Success

One of the important criticisms of the experiment (discussed more fully in chapter 6) is the fact that there exist very few output measures other than achievement tests by which to evaluate the relative performance of the companies. The interim performance objective (IPO) tests were different for each of the six programs, they were inadequately policed (see chapter 5), and they were not even given to control groups, so it is impossible to use them to compare performance either between experimental and control groups or between different companies. There were no other cognitive tests administered to the whole sample. Initially there were plans to measure student and parent attitudes before and after the experiment, but these plans were dropped. It was impossible to distribute questionnaires to all groups early enough in the program; the response rate on those distributed turned out to be very low (about 50 percent of the students for whom full test data was available); and the OEO ultimately decided that it would be too costly to send them out at the end of the school year. A survey of the teachers involved elicited only a 20 percent response rate, and in any event it included no questions on whether teachers felt the companies were successful or not.[10]

As a consequence, there were only two ways in which to obtain supportive data for the achievement test results. One somewhat rigorous method was to compare the daily attendance figures of students in the experimental and control groups. These attendance figures were recorded for most of the students who remained in the program all year and took both tests, with a measurement reliability as good as that of any other data used in the analysis. If the attendance of students in the experimental groups was systematically higher than that of students in the control groups, it might be inferred that the participating students liked school more and that the companies were in this sense successful.

10. This teachers' survey is described in an internal OEO memo by assistant project director Judy Glotzer, "Feedback on the ETS and Battelle Questionnaires," November 4, 1971.

Table 4-7. Attendances and Absences, Experimental and Control Groups, by Grade, 1970–71 School Year

Item[a]			Grade				All grades
	1	*2*	*3*	*7*	*8*	*9*	
1. Number of students in the experimental group for whom attendance records were kept	983	1,034	1,063	1,102	1,099	1,014	6,295
2. Percentage of full-year, full-test data sample	82	75	76	85	89	84	82
3. Number of students in the control group for whom attendance records were kept	721	653	758	917	884	827	4,760
4. Percentage of full-year, full-test data sample	62	56	63	77	76	78	69
5. Percentage of days absent, experimental students	7.43	6.14	6.52	7.73	8.18	8.51	7.42
6. Percentage of days absent, control students	7.55	6.55	6.76	7.08	7.98	7.82	7.29
7. Difference (control minus experimental)	0.12	0.41	0.24	−0.65	−0.20	−0.69	−0.13

Source: Same as Table 4-1.

a. The experimental sample is incomplete, mainly because attendance was not recorded in Grand Rapids, the Bronx, and for the lower grades in Portland. The attendance of students in the control group was unrecorded in Taft, Philadelphia, the Las Vegas lower grades, and the Wichita first grade.

The overall attendance comparisons are given in Table 4-7. The first four rows give numbers and percentages for the attendance data by experimental and control status. These data are somewhat incomplete because attendance records were not kept in Grand Rapids and the Bronx, for the lower grades in Portland, nor for the control groups in Taft and Philadelphia, the lower grades in the control group in Las Vegas, and the first grade in the control group in Wichita. Rows 5 and 6 give the percentages of days absent for all grades, and row 7 the differences between control and experimental percentages. These differences are invariably quite small, but they do indicate somewhat more absences in the control group in the lower grades (where students probably skip school quite rarely) and more absences in the experimental group in the upper grades (where students may skip school). If anything, then, these attendance figures suggest that students in the control group seemed to enjoy school slightly better than students in the experiment.

A regression similar to the one described above for test scores was used for the site-by-site pattern of attendance differences. The results (given in Table 4-6, column 3) indicate:

1. Two companies, Learning Foundations and Singer/Graflex, apparently were responsible for poorer attendance than in the control schools.

2. In the only indication there is that instructional cost makes any difference, daily attendance of participating students was somewhat lower in those sites where the companies did spend less than the control schools (designated by low instructional cost in Table 4-6; see also page 46, note 9).

3. Holding constant all other factors, the attendance record of the experimental group relative to the control group was better in large cities, but worse by about the same amount in all northeastern sites.

4. For some reason large losses of instructional time in the experimental programs, which could be thought of as a measure of the disturbances or chaos in a site, are associated with improved attendance of participating students.

5. As before, the fit of the regression is rather poor, indicating that sitewide attendance patterns had a very high random element.

A second, more casual way to buttress the results of the achievement tests was to interview local school personnel assigned to manage the experiment in the different sites. When these project directors were asked whether they felt the companies were in some sense more successful than the control public schools, a surprising proportion of them felt that they were. Whereas Table 4-5 indicates that the companies were more successful by a noticeable margin in only seven sites, thirteen of the eighteen project directors in company sites felt that the contractors' program was a success, that it benefited teachers and students in various ways, and they were surprised that the test scores did not show this. Opinions were split between those who felt the companies would have appeared successful if measured with criterion-referenced tests (like the IPOs) and those who felt that they would have done better had they been given more time.

These views are by no means unbiased, and probably predictable. The on-site project directors were involved in the experiment from a relatively early time, felt responsible for their students, and tried hard to make the companies' programs successful.[11] In some cases they might

11. By way of illustration, as described in chapter 3, the project director in Athens, Georgia, one of the most successful sites, indicated (in a telephone interview) that his company was not doing well until he took over, reorganized its program, and in effect made it work. This situation was unique, but still indicative of the general feelings of the project directors.

have taken it as a personal insult that the companies did not seem to do any better with their students than the control schools. Thus they might be expected to feel unsure of, and possibly even bitter toward, the negative results of the official evaluation. How much importance should be attributed to these opinions is thus a matter of conjecture. On the one hand, the whole idea of this experiment and its supposedly rigorous evaluation was to get away from the informal and impressionistic feelings of those who worked on a project and "felt" that it was good. But on the other hand, one of the disturbing factors about the experiment was that there was little besides achievement test scores upon which to base an evaluation. If these scores represent an inadequate yardstick for any reason, the supposedly objective evaluation may not be accurate.[12] This quandary is discussed in more detail in chapter 6, but it is worth noting here how ironic it is that performance contracting, demanding as it does that performance be measured in hard quantitative ways, should appear to be most successful when evaluated by a much softer and more impressionistic standard.

GENERALLY THIS EVIDENCE indicates that performance contracting was not successful. The objective evidence, whether from achievement test gains in reading or mathematics, gains in other subjects, or daily attendance records indicates little ground for enthusiasm about the contractors' performance. The mean gains in reading and mathematics adjusted

12. Although the questions on the teacher survey are so indirect and the response rate so low that it is difficult to read much into the results, they do confirm in broad outline those of the survey of project directors. The teachers, while typically rather negative about giving incentive contracts to private firms, nevertheless generally seemed to favor the instructional methods used by the firms and want them continued. (See OEO internal memo, "Feedback on the ETS and Battelle Questionnaires.")

This point, incidentally, represents the major difference between the generally negative OEO evaluation of performance contracting and the more positive Rand evaluation of five locally initiated projects. The Rand projects were not designed to include control groups and very precise pre- and post-test measurement, but were designed to look carefully for possible changes in teaching and administrative arrangements within the school. The gains shown in the first year tests—what there are of them—agree very closely with the OEO results, but Rand tempers its evaluation with the qualitative information, similar to that expressed by many OEO site directors and teachers, that performance contracting seems to be popular and to have benefited students, schools, and teachers in subtle ways. See Polly Carpenter and George R. Hall, *Case Studies in Educational Performance Contracting: Conclusions and Implications*, R-900/1–HEW (Santa Monica, Calif.: Rand Corporation, 1971).

for initial score differences suggested that students in the experiment did slightly better than they would have done in normal circumstances. But these same students, particularly those in the upper grades, had slightly worse attendance records than students in the control group and were noticeably worse in other subjects not actually taught by the companies. There is some evidence on the other side, however, from the casual and possibly biased impressions of the site project directors, that the experimental group did better than the control group.

Nor were the individual site results particularly interesting. The students of one company, Quality Educational Development Corporation, did better on the test scores by an amount that could be considered educationally significant. Another company, Westinghouse Learning Corporation, did worse than the control schools, while two other companies, Learning Foundations and Singer/Graflex, seem to have had a slightly deleterious effect on student attendance though not on test scores. There was also a mild suggestion that performance contracting worked slightly better in sites with a large Chicano student population and also in the South Central and Southeast regions.

5. Monetary Incentives in Education

Although performance contracts of one sort or another have been widely used in government procurement for a number of years, it was not until the Texarkana experience of 1969 that this technique was applied to the procurement of educational services. Until then school boards purchased their services through direct arrangements with teachers or their unions, without any significant performance incentives. One of the important outcomes of the OEO experiment therefore is to see whether it is in fact feasible to use incentive contracting in the area of education. This chapter examines this aspect of the experiment and problems arising from such contractual arrangements.

The Contracts

Government procurement contracts vary widely in the degree of incentives for good performance and also in the amount of risk undertaken by the contractor. At one extreme contracts can be of the cost-plus-fixed-fee variety, where the contractor is assured that the government will cover all of his costs as long as all specific activities are approved beforehand and as long as the contractor meets minimal output standards. Because costs and the feasibility of producing certain items on schedule are so uncertain in research and development endeavors, this type of contract is typically used in these areas. At the other extreme, contracts can be of a fixed-price variety, where the contractor is not guaranteed that the government will cover his costs but will purchase from him only a given number of units of output at a predetermined price. Since this type of contractual arrangement builds in a strong incentive for the contractor to minimize costs, it is often used in relatively routine procurement operations where the government is purchasing a known quantity with reasonably well-determined output costs. Such contracts are not very common in research and development because contractors have learned that they take unusual risks when they sign up for a fixed-price incentive arrangement without a reasonable knowledge of the cost and feasibility of producing the output.

Although performance contracting in 1970 was new and virtually untested, the educational firms bidding to take part in the OEO experiment were so confident of success and so eager to gain performance contracting business that they all signed the equivalent of fixed-priced contracts.[1] These contracts stipulated that a firm would get paid a fixed sum whenever the student gained at least one grade level in a subject, with additional payments for gains beyond this level. Even if the firm were to find it very costly to achieve this grade level gain, it was not reimbursed for these extra costs, in fact receiving no payment whatever for students who failed to achieve the minimum gain. And the firm did all this in the presence of an additional stipulation that effectively limited its profit to a maximum of 15 percent of its costs.

Although the fixed-price structure of the contracts put the firms at an immediate disadvantage, they might conceivably still have returned a profit on the venture if the minimum guarantee gain had not been so high. The guarantee was set at one grade equivalent unit by OEO for purposes of preliminary contractual negotiations, and it was only rarely bargained down from this level by the firms[2]—although later OEO did propose a generous relaxation of this provision after the experiment was over when it was clear that the firms had lost a great deal of money (see page 60). Even though firms may have been anticipating subsequent contracts as a result of their initial participation in the experiment, it remains a great mystery why they acquiesced in this provision. The threshold was so high that students had to average a gain of 1.6 grade equivalent units for the firm to break even and 1.9 units for the firm to make the maximum profit—all well above the gain that

1. As mentioned in chapter 2, these contracts were in reality signed with the local school boards. Since OEO had agreed to pay all of the school boards' contractual expenses, however, OEO actually negotiated the contracts with the firms.
2. Of the six firms, Alpha Learning Systems, Plan Education Centers, and Singer/ Graflex all had lower minimum levels in some or all of the first three elementary grades. No firms had lower minimum levels in the upper grades.

might have been expected from these students on the basis of their past performance. As seen in chapter 4, the latter expectation proved to be the more realistic—the gain for all students in the experiment ultimately averaged 0.6 grade equivalent unit on the evaluation tests and even less on the payments tests (see page 43, note 8), with less than half of them gaining 1.0 grade equivalent unit and hence eligible for any payment at all and less than 10 percent gaining the amount necessary for the firm to be paid the maximum.

The entire contractual side of the experiment was marred because the firms, either in enthusiasm or ignorance, had signed such unfavorable contracts. Whether rightly or not, the firms became very disillusioned with the whole idea of performance contracting and were not at all mollified by the rather generous final settlement of the contracts proposed by OEO. Of the six firms in the experiment, one went bankrupt, two more dropped direct classroom work, and all six stopped accepting incentive-based contracts. In August 1974—three years after the close of the experiment—three of these firms still had not reached final agreements with OEO.[3]

The issues and problems raised by this attempt to use incentive contracting in education fall into two broad classes: those involving the types of incentives that school boards might like to build into contracts to encourage certain types of teaching and those involving the detailed problems of negotiating and settling contracts. Each of these is discussed in turn.

Specific Incentive Provisions

One of the intriguing aspects of performance contracting has been the possibility that the incentive procedure would encourage specific types of teaching, focus on different groups of children, and direct attention to other similar objectives. On the positive side, this would increase

3. Of the six firms, Plan Education Centers, Westinghouse Learning Corporation, and Learning Foundations had all negotiated final settlements with OEO by April 1972, nine months after the close of the school year. Negotiations with Alpha Learning Systems and Singer/Graflex were carried on for another year without success. There have never been any serious negotiations with Quality Educational Development Corporation, ironically the company that did the best (see chapter 4). This firm was dissolved soon after the experiment ended. The latter three cases will probably eventually be turned over to the Department of Justice for litigation.

the ability of school boards to oversee the type of teaching being done. On the negative side, it could lead to unintended homogenization of teaching, to a very narrow educational focus (which is what seems to have happened in England in the last century, see page 5), and it may leave little room for imagination and independence on the part of either students or teachers.

Although the evidence is murky, there is at least some indication that the specific incentive provisions may have had some effect on the form of teaching in a locally initiated trial of performance contracting in Banneker School at Gary, Indiana, in 1970. Here a private teaching firm, Behavioral Research Laboratories (BRL), was given a performance contract to teach the entire elementary student body for three years. Parents in the neighborhood served by this school were free to send their children to other schools if they chose, and other parents in the district were free to enroll their children in Banneker. The firm was supposed to conduct all instruction in the school, though because of the difficulty in measuring gains in some subjects, the contracts stipulated that payment would be based only on achievement test scores in reading and mathematics. At the end of three years, the Gary contracts guaranteed the firm about $2,400 for every student attaining the national norms in standardized reading and mathematics tests, but—like the contracts in Texarkana and in the OEO experiment—it got nothing for the others.[4]

As the Gary project began, it became apparent that the specific provisions of the contracts were indeed influencing the teaching, unfortunately in questionable ways. Possibly because BRL was only being paid for its performance in reading and mathematics, in the first few months of the project it taught only these two subjects. This persisted until the state board of education intervened.[5]

There was also some indication of a more subtle form of discrimination. Since the Gary contracts rewarded BRL only for students achiev-

---

4. Much of this and the following material comes from a Rand Corporation report by G. R. Hall and M. L. Rapp, *Case Studies in Educational Performance Contracting: Gary, Indiana*, R-900/4–HEW (Santa Monica, Calif.: Rand Corporation, 1971).

5. Hall and Rapp note that there was little instruction in subjects other than reading and mathematics in the beginning of the experimental period, but are somewhat vague on whether this apportionment of time can actually be attributed to the incentive contracts. Conceivably BRL could merely have been slow in developing and implementing its instructional programs in these subjects (ibid., p. 25).

ing normal district levels in reading and mathematics at the end of every year, there was an incentive for the firm to teach the students in the middle of the distribution and to ignore those at the extremes. Even though Banneker was a low-ranking school academically, the very best students could achieve normal levels without a great deal of time and effort. Since the payment for these students was more or less assured, there would not be much point in BRL concentrating on them. At the other extreme, the very worst students in Banneker probably could not attain normal levels no matter what attention was given them, so there was not much point in BRL focusing on them either. The only students that it paid BRL to concentrate on—and where BRL presumably put its resources—was on the students in the middle of the distribution, who were far enough behind that they had to be taught but close enough to the average level that all effort might not be wasted. Since BRL did control the entire school, it could have used initial pretests to group students according to these categories of potential profitability and focus teaching effort accordingly.

There were no reports of anything very obvious along these lines occurring at Banneker, but an interesting analysis of the first year test scores by George Peterson suggests that there may have been some subtle influences at work.[6] Compared with a national sample of students, reading and mathematics improvement at Banneker appeared to be somewhat better for students in the middle of the distribution and somewhat less at either extreme. There was also a somewhat greater propensity for students in the middle of the distribution to reenroll for a second year compared with students at the extremes. While there could have been other causes for these phenomena—in particular, the instructional programs may not have been fully developed for the upper-bracket students—this is at least suggestive evidence that the special incentive provisions of performance contracting could be important and should be watched carefully.

Although there were also specific incentives in the OEO contracts, including some OEO itself later came to regret,[7] it is doubtful that for

6. George E. Peterson, "The Distributional Impact of Performance Contracting in Schools," in Harold M. Hochman and George E. Peterson (eds.), *Redistribution through Public Choice* (Columbia University Press, published in cooperation with the Urban Institute, 1974), pp. 129–33.

7. See U.S. Office of Economic Opportunity, Office of Planning, Research, and Evaluation, *An Experiment in Performance Contracting: Summary of Preliminary Results,* OEO Pamphlet 3400-5 (1972), p. 29.

at least the one year of the experiment they could have been very significant determinants of the pattern of student improvement. For one thing, the OEO contracts were different from the Gary contracts in that they rewarded achievement gains and not post-year levels, which meant that it would have been much more difficult for the firms to identify promising students. Secondly, in the OEO experiment the firms were not in charge of the entire school but only their own classrooms, which meant that there was much less scope for grouping students, focusing programs, and other forms of discrimination. Almost all observers agree that it would have been difficult to do this in any but the most subtle ways within the classrooms—especially when, as with these performance contracting programs, the curriculum instruction relied so heavily on the initiative of individual students.

But even though the odds are against any sort of subtle focusing of this sort, it is still worthwhile to examine this question empirically, if for no other reason than that it is so important and has received so much attention. The OEO contracts, perhaps unwisely, made no payments for students who failed to gain a grade equivalent unit in an academic year and conferred a bonus for student gains in excess of this grade equivalent level. If these provisions had any effect, they would encourage firms to single out the students most likely to gain a grade equivalent unit or more and maximize the gains for these students. Conversely, if the firms found during the course of the year (say, from the interim tests they conducted themselves) that some students were not gaining at a fast enough rate to reach the grade level minimum, there would be little point in spending more money on these students. Compared with students in the control groups, therefore, one might expect the variance of the gains of the experimental students to be greater, because the firms would magnify the gains of the big gainers and minimize the gains of the low gainers.

This hypothesis was tested by comparing the variance of gains of the experimental groups to the variance of gains for the control groups. Table 5-1 presents the ratios of these variances for the entire sample of 14,650 students at school for the full year who took all the tests.

The performance incentives appear to have little effect on the pattern of gains. Of the twelve possible cases (reading and mathematics in each of six grades), experimental group gains had a greater variance in seven, with the difference being statistically significant in four of these cases. The average variance across all grades was greater by a barely significant margin in the experimental groups in reading but smaller in

Table 5-1. Ratio of the Variance of Gains of the Experimental Group to Those of the Control Group in the Educational Performance Contracting Experiment, by Subject and Grade, 1970–71 School Year

| | Grade | | | | | | |
Subject	1	2	3	7	8	9	Average
Reading	0.947	1.090[a]	1.095[a]	1.151[a]	1.065	0.995	1.057[a]
Mathematics	1.057	0.722	1.059	0.893	0.820	1.353[a]	0.984
Both subjects	1.002	0.906	1.077[a]	1.022	0.942	1.174[a]	1.020

Source: Derived from test data provided by Battelle Columbus Laboratories on the Office of Economic Opportunity experiment in educational performance contracting, 1970–71 school year.
a. Significantly greater than unity at the 95 percent confidence level.

mathematics. Across the two subjects the experimental variance was significantly greater in two of the six grades but also significantly smaller in two grades. For all students across all grades and subjects the variance of experimental gains was virtually identical to that of the control groups.

Nor is there evidence either of a greater variance of experimental gains on a site-by-site basis. Of the 236 site-grade-subject possibilities, there were only 27 instances of significantly greater experimental variances, 90 instances of insignificantly greater experimental variances, and 119 instances of smaller experimental variances. A regression fit to these variance ratios in the manner adopted in chapter 4 indicated no systematic patterns whatever in these results. No matter how the variances are analyzed, therefore, there is no evidence suggesting that the specific incentives of the OEO contracts had any effects.

This should not be taken to mean that the problem is unimportant. If firms had more power to group students by prospective profitability, the information on which to make such groupings, and more time, specific incentives might well make a difference. And if that were the case, contracts such as the ones used by OEO that encouraged firms to ignore the least promising gainers would have a definite perverse influence. A preferable instrument would be one that rewarded the additional learning of every student—that imposed no threshold level of gain as a condition of payment.

Beyond that, if school districts ever use performance contracting on a large scale, the contracts should reflect the type of teaching that the districts want. In the OEO case the goal of the incentive instruction was more or less that of compensatory education programs: to raise the academic skills of underprivileged students in reading and mathematics. Apart from technical deficiencies such as the threshold gain problem mentioned above, an incentive system that might ultimately be preferable to the one used in the OEO experiment would be to reward achievement gains more, the more underprivileged the student. Defining underprivileged status would raise the same sort of difficulties it now raises in allocating funds for compensatory education (should slow learners or impoverished students be assisted?), but even crude efforts at specifying the preferred recipients of compensatory programs may be better than none at all.[8]

Contractual Problems in Education

Even if these philosophical questions were satisfactorily resolved, there would still exist another and possibly more difficult set of issues. Just as specific incentives ultimately raise the question of which subjects the school board wants taught and which students it wants aided, the idea of educational contracting forces school boards to make and negotiate a whole range of minor decisions that are generally the province of school principals and teachers. One of the lessons of the OEO experience is that this may not be a viable arrangement. Certainly the number of ambiguities in the initial payments contracts indicates that both OEO and the educational firms were quite unaware of all the difficulties that would arise.

The first and most serious difficulty concerned lost instructional time. Though the initial contracts specified that the firms would have 160 hours of instructional time in both reading and mathematics (one hour a day for 180 days minus ten days' allowance for testing at the beginning and end of the year), they actually had a good deal less. There were normal disturbances, such as fire drills and assemblies, and abnormal disturbances, such as teacher strikes. Students were frequently absent. In many schools, "class hours" were only fifty minutes, and some were as short as forty minutes. While these factors could have been anticipated in the initial negotiations, the wording of the contracts was

8. Many of these issues are discussed by Donald Richard in "Performance Contracting for Equal Opportunity and School System Renewal" (Harvard University, 1971; processed).

vague and OEO eventually proposed a rather generous settlement to try to resolve the inevitable contractual disputes. For purposes of computing student payments, OEO offered to multiply all gains by the factor:

$$\frac{165}{\text{Actual average full}} \times \frac{60}{\text{Actual class}}.$$
$$\text{time attendance in site} \quad \text{minutes in site}$$

This adjustment in effect guaranteed perfect student attendance up to 165 days, that allowance for testing would be less than initially supposed, that all class hours would be sixty minutes (in fact, if the minute average was between fifty and sixty, it was rounded down to fifty), and that all realized achievement gains would be prorated across the lost instructional time. The average instructional time inflation factor across all sites was 1.5, and it was as high as 2.1 in one site. This effectively lowered the average grade level guarantee in the contracts to 0.7— roughly the median gain for all students. Since many more students were now eligible for payment, this later adjustment alone raised firm payments by about 80 percent.[9] Though, with the benefit of hindsight, one might question whether the adjustment was not overly generous, the contractual guarantees were already so high that such a change did make the contracts more realistic. And even with such a generous adjustment, OEO still has not had an easy time reaching final settlement (witness the three firms that still had not been settled).

A similar problem existed with students who did not attend the experimental program for the full year. Students who dropped out or who were not given the tests either before or after the school year for the usual reasons, such as illness or transfer, would not cause any problem in analyzing the evaluation test results as long as they did not differ systematically from those for the students in the experimental group who took all tests—attrition would then be the same as not testing a random sample of experimental students. But this attrition would cause problems in computing the firms' payments because the firms were

9. See Charles B. Stalford, "Contractual Procedures," in U.S. Office of Economic Opportunity, Office of Planning, Research, and Evaluation, *An Experiment in Performance Contracting,* OEO Pamphlet 3400-6 (1972), p. 146, and *Evaluation of the Office of Economic Opportunity's Performance Contracting Experiment,* Report to the Congress by the Comptroller General of the United States, B-130515 (1973), pp. 63–68.

paid according to the number of students who gained a grade equivalent unit. The initial plan (described in chapter 2) was to replace departing students from a pool of replacement students, testing both as they left or entered the experimental program, and then splicing together the achievement gains. However, this plan proved unworkable because students often dropped out without warning and could not be tested, because the replacement pool of students was itself depleted by attrition from both the experimental and replacement groups during the summer preceding the experiment, and because toward the end of the year the parents of students in the replacement pool became increasingly reluctant to have their children join a temporary teaching program for a few months. Thus, to compensate for this underenrollment of full-time students, the average gains of those students in the experiment full time had to be prorated again to compute average gains for contractual purposes.

Another difficult problem concerned the interim performance objective (IPO) tests. The contracts based up to 25 percent of the firms' payment on the proportion of students who passed five of these criterion-referenced tests (intended to measure mastery of specific curricular skills), on the grounds that the standard achievement test measures might not give a complete indication of the contractors' success. But the questions on criterion-referenced tests were geared to individual firms' instructional programs, which logically implies that each firm should be allowed to give its own tests. This is obviously infeasible when firm payments are to be based on how well firms do on the same tests, and certain ground rules were necessary. What was ultimately decided, and unfortunately also proved completely unworkable, was for the firms to submit their tests to the presumably impartial evaluation contractor, Battelle Memorial Institute, for prior approval before administering the tests. This procedure broke down when it became apparent that there would not be time for firms to construct tests on the basis of instructional content, submit them to Battelle for approval, administer them, and repeat the procedure four more times during the year. Consequently the firms constructed and gave their own tests, sometimes gaining Battelle certification later and sometimes not, and getting a much better financial settlement here than on the evaluation based on official payments tests. According to the General Accounting Office, the firms' payments under the IPO test provisions were 73 percent of their maximum earnings, compared with 33 percent for the payments tests, or 59 percent after the OEO adjustment for lost instructional time.[10] Another irony of the experience then is that an experiment which began with such concern about "teaching to the tests" should have ended up by basing payments on this procedure that represents the extreme case. It is even more ironic, and mysterious, that all firms did not attain the full payments on their interim tests.

There is a long list of other contractual problems that arose in the course of the experiment. As discussed in chapter 3, conditions in two sites, the Bronx and in the upper grades at Philadelphia, were so chaotic that for payments purposes OEO disregarded the incentive payments provisions altogether and settled on a straight-cost reimbursable basis. Since the pretest for the first grade, and in some cases the second grade, was too difficult for many of the students, so that grade equivalent rankings were not accurate, these gains were computed on the basis of an arbitrary calculation of how well students might have done had there been tests that were accurate in this range.[11] At the other extreme, there were some students who achieved the maximum grade equivalent score on the post-test, which meant that they might have done even better had there been more accurate tests in this range. For these few students, OEO dropped the minimum grade level guarantee and simply paid according to average gains realized in the classroom. Finally, because most of the firms failed to earn 80 percent of their maximum earnings (which OEO had already advanced to cover firms' cash flow requirements), and because five of the six firms eventually were unable to obtain payment bonds as collateral against the OEO advance, the contractual negotiations typically took the form of OEO trying to get some of its money back.[12] This created an incentive for the firms to be difficult to locate at settlement time, which in fact three of them were.

THE ATTEMPT TO USE INCENTIVE CONTRACTING in the education area has thus proved to be rather inauspicious. The firms involved with OEO had very little idea of how well they could perform and signed contracts that turned out to be quite unfavorable. The specific incentives built into the contracts would, if they had had any effects at all, have en-

---

10. *Evaluation of the Office of Economic Opportunity's Performance Contracting Experiment*, pp. 68–69.

11. This problem was not as serious for the raw scores used in the evaluation tests because students at least received a pretest score.

12. See Stalford, "Contractual Procedures," pp. 148–50.

couraged firms to ignore those students least capable of improvement—representing a somewhat questionable policy for compensatory education. Further, even such an apparently straightforward matter as paying firms according to how well students do in reading and mathematics raised a host of legal questions regarding inevitable losses of instruction time, part-year students, testing difficulties, and assorted problems and disturbances during the school year. One can only imagine the troubles that might ensue if this procedure were extended to areas where it would be more difficult to evaluate progress. And, finally, the difficulty that OEO, with its large program and legal staff, has had in reaching agreements with the contractors raises the specter of school boards around the country tied up in endless litigation with educational contractors, paying large sums in legal fees, and probably eventually being forced to make quite expensive settlements. There may yet be some hope for incentive contracting in education, but the difficulties experienced in that experiment, and the speed with which the idea has been dropped in these and other sites around the country, indicate that school boards and firms both should be wary of such arrangements.

6. Performance Contracting and the Strategy of Experimentation

Unlike other social experiments in income maintenance, housing, and health care, educational experiments are directed to changing policy at the state and local, not the federal, levels. The federal government has the financial resources and expertise necessary to do experiments, it can initiate projects in different sites and geographic areas, and it can command greater publicity than its state and local counterparts. But its role must be limited to determining interesting areas for experimentation, reporting results, and providing financial assistance or legislative inducements to encourage the adoption of promising new policies. For the most part it is up to state and local governments, or specifically their school boards, to determine how the results of an experiment are to be used.

The performance contracting experience demonstrates this divided federal, state, and local responsibility. The idea first arose as a result of the Texarkana project, which was locally initiated and federally funded. It captured the attention of both the educational community and federal policymakers, creating sufficient support for the concept that the Office of Economic Opportunity decided to do the large-scale experiment described in this study. Although possibly reflecting a serious mistake in design, the OEO experiment was over in a year, which implied that the information it generated could still be of current interest to local school boards. The main problem, which probably accounts for the dissatisfaction with the experiment, was that performance contracting itself did not appear to work very well.

It should be recognized that the strategy of social experimentation necessarily implies that many of the policies under examination will not work. This, after all, is precisely the reason for such a strategy—since there is uncertainty about how programs will work once put in the field, it makes sense to run a test of the program with a control population to see what can be learned. If the program appears to work, it can be improved and expanded; if it does not, it can be set aside, without the interference of supporting interest groups who could otherwise keep it going if it had been established on a large scale.

But granting the logical possibility that some programs are bound to fail, as a practical matter program failure is disappointing for two important reasons—because there is an urgent need to find programs that will succeed, and because there is also uncertainty about the strategy of experimenting with policies. Since techniques for conducting such experiments and for measuring outcomes are admittedly still very crude, there is a great risk that imperfect experiments with new policy measures or educational procedures will lead to programs being discarded that may in fact be good measures if only techniques and evaluation procedures were improved. Good programs in education or any other area of social policy are rare. It is a loss if even a few promising candidates are eliminated for the wrong reasons. This is why whenever a promising program does not appear to work well, as performance contracting did not, the experiment must be examined just as carefully as the policy measure itself to minimize the danger that improper conclusions are being drawn from the experience.

With these considerations in mind, this chapter first reviews several important criticisms of the experiment that were lodged at different stages of the project, particularly the extent to which any defects in the design of the experiment might have led to misleading inferences about performance contracting. How the experiment was received and might have affected the educational policies of local school boards is considered next. And, finally, the question is asked: What has the project to say in more general terms about the advantages and limitations of social experiments in education?

Major Shortcomings

The major criticisms leveled at the OEO project questioned its basic objectives, how it was evaluated, and how it was conducted.

The Goal of the Project

A fundamental shortcoming of the performance contracting experiment concerned the confusion over the basic goal of the enterprise. As mentioned in chapter 2, the underlying concept of performance contracting could have been tested in two quite different ways: either to determine whether private firms with 1970 vintage technology could teach better than traditional schools, or to determine whether economic and contractual incentives would in the long run encourage better teaching and would therefore be a preferable means for local school boards to purchase educational services than the current procedures. There was confusion about these two partially incompatible objectives from the outset. As it was ultimately designed, the experiment represented an uneasy compromise between the two, not altogether satisfactory from either standpoint. It was like a test of contractual incentives in that contracts were signed and used, and both experimental companies and control schools were free to vary their instructional methods, but unlike such a test in being limited to a relatively short period of time.

Although the confusion of objectives was regrettable and should have been avoided, it may not have been too damaging and might even have been in a peculiar sort of way advantageous. The experiment was not designed to test precisely either the incentive system or the instructional methods of contractors, but it did generate some information on both questions and might, therefore, have served better than if it only generated information on one question or the other.

To be more specific, since the experiment lasted only one year, it gave almost no information regarding the long-run effectiveness of a well-designed system of contractual incentives in education. At the same time, a system of contractual incentives was negotiated with the contractors and, as documented in chapter 5, attempting to organize this system for a short period taught everybody a great deal about it—mainly that although the idea of introducing market incentives into education is an appealing one, such a system is tremendously difficult to develop and implement. It is not easy to write contracts that encourage companies to focus on objectives school boards consider desirable. Decisions have to be made on how much to reward students' progress in basic reading and mathematics skills relative to progress in other subjects, on how to reward cognitive gains relative to other measures such as student attitudes and enthusiasm, on what tests to use to measure such progress, on how to reward the progress of smart and easy-to-teach students as opposed to that of the unresponsive. Once these issues are resolved, there are a host of subsidiary contractual questions regarding proper choices of tests, adjustments for testing difficulties, adjustments for absences or lost instructional time, part-year students, and so forth. Then, to avoid the costly and unending litigation that took place after the experiment, and the generous concessions that had to be made, all of these issues must be clearly resolved before the contracts are first signed. These difficulties are not necessarily insuperable, but they should at least be revealed to school districts before they enter into performance contracts on their own. From this standpoint the OEO experiment, although it was very poorly designed to test a system of contractual incentives, did at least generate useful information about the pitfalls to be avoided in signing incentive contracts.

By the same token, even though the experiment was not well suited to measure the efficacy of various instructional methods, a crude comparison of the achievement test score gains of students operating under different programs could be made. There proved to be only slight differences between the achievement gains of students in the experimental classrooms, which tended to rely on individualized methods of instruction, teaching machines, paraprofessionals, and student incentives, and students in the control classrooms, who were generally taught in more traditional ways. Nor were there large differences in the results for different companies, although some, such as Learning Foundations and Westinghouse Learning Corporation, began the year using much less traditional methods than other companies, such as Plan Education Centers and the local teacher organizations (although as noted in chapter 3, these differences abated during the year). The lack of control and documentation of the teaching methods used in the experiment make it impossible to go beyond these general statements or to say why programs did or did not work, but the uniformity of results suggests that if one is prepared to measure and compare teaching ability by achievement test gains alone, the different instructional methods used in this experiment do not appear to affect the findings very much.

Tests and Measurement

But perhaps one should not rely solely on achievement test gains as a measure of the desirability of instructional programs. This brings up a second serious problem with the experiment. It was noted in chapter 4 that many project directors "felt" that the companies' performance was more successful than the test results showed. At one level, many argued that the evaluation should have been done with criterion-referenced tests measuring mastery of specific skills, rather than with achievement tests designed primarily to screen above-average students from below-average students.[1] More fundamentally, it can be argued that in education, unlike other program areas, no one really knows how to measure success: whether to identify good students from bad students or to identify good programs from bad programs. Although there is certainly no consensus on goals, it is generally acknowledged that education should equip students to become contented, respected, and intelligent citizens earning reasonably high incomes and with an active interest in community affairs. It is obviously impossible to measure these adult traits when students are still students, and so the educational system has resorted to a series of proxy measures to identify the promising among the mediocre students and also the promising among the mediocre educational programs. But these measures, uniformly emphasizing cognitive ability, have never been thoroughly validated in the sense that it is not clear that high test scores alone can indicate much about success or happiness in adult life.[2] Thus, if one were to take a somewhat more agnostic view of achievement tests, one might not be too upset if certain educational programs such as those used by the performance contractors did not lead to significant gains.

In its extreme form this agnostic view would not leave much future for educational experiments or research of any kind. Since it has not been established that any existing student measurement device is well correlated with adult success, there is in principle no way of identifying promising from unpromising educational programs, and no point in even trying them out. Educational policy research is then put in a straitjacket which cannot be removed until that time, long in the future, when there

1. For a good statement of this position as it pertains to the locally initiated performance contracting projects, see Polly Carpenter and George R. Hall, *Case Studies in Educational Performance Contracting: Conclusions and Implications,* R-900/1–HEW (Santa Monica, Calif.: Rand Corporation, 1971), p. 17.

2. In fact, many observers think they indicate very little about adult welfare. See, for example, Christopher Jencks and others, *Inequality: A Reassessment of the Effect of Family and Schooling in America* (Basic Books, 1972); David C. McClelland, "Testing for Competence Rather Than for 'Intelligence,'" *American Psychologist,* vol. 28 (January 1973), pp. 1–14; and Finis Welch, "Relationships between Income and Schooling" (City University of New York, Graduate School, January 1973; processed).

is a consensus about what constitutes adult success and what student measurement device can best predict success.

But this view is undoubtedly pessimistic, and perhaps even destructive. There may be doubts about a particular set of cognitive tests, but it would be most extraordinary if adult success were completely unrelated to the cognitive abilities of students. Surely students who can read at an early age have a better chance at a more satisfactory adult life than students who cannot. And surely efforts to teach and measure student reading ability should not be abandoned until it is proved they serve no purpose. Beyond this, though there may be uncertainty about any one particular measurement instrument, local school boards can surely select teachers, instructional programs, and the like, using any criteria that appeal to them, including the casual impressions of participants on whether they are effective. There must be some choices that appear better than others in several ways, and it would surely be unwise not to adopt them just because they cannot yet be precisely evaluated.

These ideas surface in several aspects of this particular educational experiment. The purpose of the performance contracting experiment was to find a better way to teach disadvantaged students reading and mathematics, which is a worthy goal even though it may be difficult to measure the degree of improvement achieved. But there is sufficient uncertainty about the meaning of any one particular type of test that the experiment undoubtedly would have benefited if there had been more ways of measuring the success or failure of the various instructional methods. The simple device of giving more achievement tests would have reduced the possibility that apparent gains or losses were due to abnormal testing conditions—in the experiment this could easily have been done by giving the payments tests to the control group as well as the experimental group of students. Criterion-referenced tests, such as the interim performance objective tests, could also have been administered to both groups, under tightened conditions of approval and standardization, to determine whether students in experimental classrooms progressed at all in terms of their absolute mastery of specific skills. There could have been more extensive attempts to measure attitudes, social interaction, initiative, and behavior to see if participating students were in some sense happier or more enthusiastic than students in the control classrooms. There could also have been a much more serious effort to interview local teachers, principals, and other school personnel to see if their impressions confirmed the test results (which they may not have if the survey of project directors undertaken for this study is any guide).

From this perspective the ideal performance contracting experiment would be designed to provide local school boards with a much broader range of evaluative information. The government would inform school boards of the project and then would simply make available results for each company on each dimension at the close of the project. There would presumably be minimal initial screening of companies—any firm that wanted to participate should be allowed to do so unless obviously unsuited—and little emphasis on reporting results for a block of companies, as in the overall comparisons for this study. Since the firms would be measured in various ways, local school boards could pick their own preferred programs on the basis of this information— much as a consumer selects a product on the basis of a range of information about it—and it would not be necessary for the government to decide which particular output measures to advertise or emphasize. An experiment set up along these lines might not achieve any more success in the purely cognitive domain, but it would be much better structured to give local school boards the information they might want.

Timing and Implementation

A final problem also suggested by some project directors as a reason why the experiment may not have been an entirely accurate test concerns whether or not companies had sufficient time to implement their instructional programs. This is a two-dimensional question: did the companies have time before the start of the experiment to set up their programs, and even if they did, was one year long enough for them to develop a smoothly running program? It was noted in chapter 3 that the experiment was launched in an incredibly short period of time. The firms did not receive an invitation to bid for the contracts until four months before they were to begin teaching, and they were not officially selected until two months before. Though at the time this was not felt to be a problem because the firms maintained that they were ready, the initial chaos in several sites indicated that this contention was far from correct. Possibly if the firms had not at the same time been trying to convince OEO of their experience and readiness so that they would be chosen to participate, they would have given a more accurate assessment of their actual ability to start the project.

There were also time pressures on the selection of local school districts. These were not named until June 1970, after summer vacation had already begun for the teachers and principals taking part in the experiment. It was then difficult for the firms to hire teachers and take other steps necessary to get the project going, and impossible for either the firms or OEO to involve any local personnel. In all likelihood the companies' programs would have done better had they had more of a chance to develop this initial cooperation.

Finally, even if there had been sufficient time at the outset for firms and school districts to plan their programs, it is most unlikely that one year is ever long enough to test fairly such a complicated operation as bringing an outside group into a public school for part-time teaching. There are inevitable conflicts of classroom and teacher scheduling which cannot be anticipated at the outset and must be resolved over time. There are inevitable problems of matching students with instructional materials, making sure that adequate supplies are available, identifying good and poor teachers and materials, and motivated and unmotivated students. Even though all companies said they could achieve dramatic gains in one year's time, these claims should have been discounted.

It is difficult to know how much the haste with which programs were launched and tested might have interfered with their success. One indication comes from an examination of the experience with several locally initiated trials with performance contracting also begun in the 1970–71 academic year, but continued for at least one extra year. These locally initiated projects did not have nearly as complete a testing program as the OEO experiment, and it is difficult to compare student gains with those of control students or with those of the same students a year earlier. The fragmentary evidence on test gains that does exist has been evaluated by the Rand Corporation, however, and its tentative conclusion is that while almost all experimental students gained at about the rate of OEO's students in the experimental (and control) groups during the 1970–71 school year, most of those that were retested seemed to do better in the subsequent year, gaining on the order of one grade equivalent unit. None of the programs reached their initial goal of doubling or tripling normal gains, however, and some programs did worse than in the previous year,[3] a not uncommon finding in educational research.

If these fragmentary results are any guide, it would clearly have been

3. The 1970–71 gains are given in Carpenter and Hall, *Case Studies in Educational Performance Contracting: Conclusions and Implications,* table 4. The fragmentary evidence concerning 1971–72 gains comes from G. R. Hall, P. Carpenter, M. L. Rapp, and G. C. Sumner, *The Evolution of Educational Performance Contracting in Five School Districts, 1971–72,* WN-7958–HEW (Santa Monica, Calif.: Rand Corporation, 1972). See especially chapters 2, 5, and 6 on Norfolk, Virginia; Gilroy, California; and Grand Rapids, Michigan.

better to test the instructional programs of the contractors with a multi-year experiment. Indeed, given all the problems that were encountered in the first, one might even consider it remarkable that inexperienced private firms did as well as the experienced regular classroom teachers in such a short time. Although a longer-term experiment would have been more costly, might have made it more difficult to enlist sites, and would have undoubtedly created many more legal and contractual problems, it has proven so difficult to make real progress in improving the educational experience of disadvantaged students that it seems worth the extra effort to try hard for the small additional gains suggested by the Rand evaluation. Even small gains, if they persist year after year, could ultimately make big dents in the academic deficiencies of disadvantaged students.

Effect of the Experiment on Educational Policies

Social experiments are intended to influence government policy, and it is important to ask whether this in fact happened with the performance contracting experiment. Since the policymaking audience for the experiment consisted of the myriads of local school districts around the country, the real question then is whether these districts seem to have been affected by the generally negative rating OEO gave performance contracting, both in terms of the disappointing achievement gains and the difficulties of incentive contracting. This reaction can be traced by looking first at the initial publicity which greeted OEO's first report on the results and then at what seems to have happened at the local level.

The post-testing for the experiment was done in June 1971, and the data stored, processed, and analyzed in the succeeding months. By late January 1972 the first report of Battelle, the evaluator, was available for release, as was a companion document provided by OEO.[4] These

---

4. The two documents are Battelle Columbus Laboratories, *Interim Report on the Office of Economic Opportunity Experiment in Educational Performance Contracting* (Columbus, Ohio: Battelle Memorial Institute, 1972); and U.S. Office of Economic Opportunity, Office of Planning, Research, and Evaluation, *An Experiment in Performance Contracting: Summary of Preliminary Results,* OEO Pamphlet 3400-5 (1972).

The local school personnel felt that this seven-month delay in reporting results was unduly long, especially because they intended to rely on the results for diagnostic information on students and also for determining whether to renew their contracts

two documents, both of which emphasized the fact that the experimental students did not seem to do any better than the control students no matter how the test results were examined, were greeted with some criticism in the press and educational community, but by no means an unusual amount. There was a spate of newspaper stories in the first two weeks of February, some critical and some laudatory editorials in the major newspapers, some subsequent criticisms and defenses in educational journals, but then interest in the issue gradually subsided. One illustration of how much interest in the controversy had died down was the fact that the critical audit of the experiment by the General Accounting Office in May 1973 received very little notice.[5]

The series of articles and comments raised almost every conceivable fair and unfair criticism of the experiment. There was criticism of OEO for wasting $6 million on a white elephant, and defense of OEO for saving local school boards possibly much more than that. There was support of OEO for the strict control group structure of the experiment, but criticism for failing to randomize selection. There was criticism by the contractors for setting up a program they alleged was intended to embarrass them, and criticism by the GAO for the procedures that resulted in the selection of these particular contractors. There was criticism for the fact that the experiment lasted only one year, and criticism that it should not have cost so much. There was criticism that the OEO evaluation disagreed with the Rand evaluation noted above, even though the differences between the two reports were mainly semantic.

Most of these criticisms have already been discussed in one way or another. While there undoubtedly were serious problems with the experiment, it does seem to have led to generally appropriate conclusions about performance contracting—that it is extremely difficult to implement such a system, and that the educational gains are not large

---

with the private firms. A Seattle teachers' union even filed a court suit to try to force earlier reporting on the results. Whether the delays were too long or not, the seven-month period was not long enough for either Battelle or OEO to analyze the results in as much detail as they would have liked, and indeed the analysts were still changing their minds about the findings up to the last minute.

5. Performance contracting stories appeared on the major news wires, and in the *New York Times, Washington Post, Wall Street Journal, Chicago Tribune, San Francisco Examiner and Chronicle,* and several other newspapers. Editorials appeared in the *Times* and *Post.* The audit by the General Accounting Office was reported in some of these papers, but much less prominently and without any extensive editorial attention.

and possibly not even positive. Whether due to the experiment or not, the influence of incentive contracting in education suffered a very fast turnaround from the time in 1970 when it seemed to be sweeping the country. Only one of the twenty OEO sites (Grand Rapids) signed a performance contract in the year following the experiment, and none have performance contracts now. The same has been true in the locally initiated projects analyzed by the Rand Corporation, which have now generally been converted to cost-plus arrangements if the contractor is still there at all.[6] Even the Banneker school in Gary, the most publicized and extensive illustration of performance contracting, closed down the program of the Behavioral Research Laboratories in the fall of 1972, a year ahead of schedule, because of the same contractual and educational problems encountered in the OEO experience. The only persisting interest involves writing incentive contracts with teachers, which many school districts are still attempting.[7]

One way in which the experiment may have given a less accurate verdict was on teaching methods. Although by the objective standards of the experiment, the individualized instruction methods used by the contractors did not appear to be highly successful, there were, as discussed above, many problems of timing, implementation, and testing encountered in the experiment. With more time, more care in adapting the contractors' programs to the needs of local teachers and students, and possibly a different type of testing, the programs used by the contractors could be developed into effective compensatory reading and mathematics programs. Some of the project directors believe that this is so and report that their districts are generally making their instructional methods more individualized. The experiment gave them valuable experience.[8]

6. See Hall and others, *Evolution of Educational Performance Contracting.*

7. The gradual disappearance of performance contracting does not mean that the idea of making schools and teachers accountable for student performance has suffered a similar fate. In fact, some seventeen states have legislative or administrative mandates to develop performance-based teacher training and certification standards, and Michigan has even gone so far as to pass a law which made local compensatory education grants conditional on the schools' ability to raise student test scores (similar to the English system in the nineteenth century). Due to political pressure from districts that would have lost money, however, the incentive provision has never been made operational—this form of performance contracting exists only on paper. For an account, see Jerome T. Murphy and David K. Cohen, "Accountability in Education—the Michigan Experience," *Public Interest,* no. 36 (Summer 1974), pp. 53–81.

8. When the local school district officially purchases the instructional materials

Lessons for the Future

After a decade of efforts to design and implement social action programs, it is now obvious that much is not known about the process of social policy formulation. The value of experiments such as this is to try out promising ideas on a small scale, under reasonably scientific conditions, in order to determine how well a policy works before and not after it is installed. In the case at hand, it seems far better to have OEO experiment with performance contracting, find that there are real problems with it, and report this information to local school boards, than to have school boards across the country plunge into performance contracting on their own, only to find out about the real problems later.

Although the experimental strategy made sense in this context, one of the important lessons of the experience is that the experimental strategy is no panacea. The OEO project showed how tremendously difficult it is to do good experiments, even ones as relatively straightforward as this. The experiment encountered difficulties at almost every stage—there were problems in determining exactly what was to be tested; in design; in selecting firms, school districts, and schools; in writing and negotiating contracts; in developing the instructional programs; in enlisting the cooperation of local personnel; and in measuring the success of the contractors. Any one of the problems, if even slightly aggravated, could have completely frustrated the enterprise. Thus the first important lesson from the experience is that social scientists should be modest about their ability to perform experiments, at least in the area of education. Experiments can be done, but they are much more difficult than the early rhetoric implied.

On a more fundamental level, the experiment leads to an even more

---

of the contractor, the program is said to be "turnkeyed." This term, originating in the world of public housing where private contractors build housing projects and turn the key over to the housing authority, was one of the original, if somewhat inconsistent, aims of those interested in performance contracting. It is very common to find a long treatise advertising the wonders of introducing incentives into education, followed by a statement that the instructional methods can ultimately be turnkeyed, which of course eliminates these incentives. (See, for example, Charles Blaschke, *Performance Contracting: Who Profits Most?* [Bloomington, Ill.: Phi Delta Kappa Educational Foundation, 1972].) This inconsistency is another example of the confusion between performance contracting as an incentive mechanism and performance contracting as an instructional method, which characterized the whole project.

humbling conclusion. Just as it is becoming clear how difficult it is to do seemingly straightforward experiments, it now appears that straightforward remedies to the educational problems of disadvantaged students simply do not exist. The initial hope of this project was that the introduction of some combination of learning technology from private industry and short-run economic incentives were the missing ingredients in previous programs to improve compensatory education. But this hope now seems naive, not only because it is not easy to add these ingredients, but also because it is now obvious that many other ingredients are missing as well. One can only speculate on what they are—whether the real breakthroughs, if they ever come, will be generated by improved instructional programs; improved training and selection of teachers; smaller and more or less structured classrooms; improved matching of teachers, programs, and students; improved diagnostic and problem-solving abilities on the part of schools; or even more fundamental changes, such as giving parents more control over their children's education. Whatever the most promising approaches turn out to be, however, it will take more careful and intensive examination than this experiment provides to find them.

All of this leads to a somewhat mixed evaluation of the prospects for experimentation in education. On the one hand, the OEO experiment did in some sense work: it showed that projects of this type can at least be completed, and it generated a great deal of knowledge both about performance contracting and about experimentation. On the other hand, it is now clear that further progress will not come without more fundamental improvements in understanding the process of learning, the workings of schools, the characteristics of successful teaching, and other difficult matters. Thus although first-generation experiments like performance contracting have played a useful role, mainly in teaching negative lessons, they do not give much promise of leading to more positive breakthroughs in the teaching of disadvantaged children.